PROPHETS AMONG US

PROPHETS AMONG US

A GUIDE FOR TRAINING PROPHETS

ISBN-13: 978-0692958612
ISBN-10: 0692958614

Cover Design by: Westley Roderick
Interior Design by: C. Rayne Warne

www.empoweredlifechurch.org
www.ivanroman.org

ACKNOWLEDGEMENTS

I would like to dedicate this book first to my wife and my boys.
You are my why.

To Empowered Life Church for loving people so well.

Lastly, to all my fellow prophetic types. Hang in there,
God is bringing a greater awareness of our role to the church.
You belong. You are needed. You are valued.

Love to you all.

ENDORSEMENTS

In every generation, the Holy Spirit raises up "Voices that Can Be Heard." These choice people carry three distinctives: 1) Biblical content, 2) gifted and empowered by the Holy Spirit and 3) character to carry the gift. I see these three elements brought together in the life and ministry of Ivan Roman. Will you find these truths woven within his book, *Prophets Among Us?* Well, if that is a question that needs an answer, then from the fruit I see in Ivan's life, the answer unequivocally is "Yes!"

Dr. James W Goll, International Speaker, Author, Recording Artist, and Founder of God Encounters Ministries

The world knows psychics and the world knows mediums but it's time for the world to engage God's voice through His people! I love that Ivan is restoring the dignity and voice of the modern prophetic office. Presidents, celebrities, and business leaders are all curious to see if God really cares about their work, their passion, or their families. God is raising up prophets in our generation to share His intention and desire with them in unique and intimate ways. Everything that happened in the Old Testament through prophets did not get down-graded when Jesus came but only increased in power and impact. When we have a right understanding of the prophetic office, then we can empower one of the most unique gift sets and personalities in the church to help have its voice and we will never be the same again. To have the church without the prophetic is like having a movie without a soundtrack; there is not the depth of experience that could be had if we align this amazing gift. Ivan has helped do that through this amazing book: *Prophets Among Us*.

Shawn Bolz, Minister, TV Personality, and Author of *Translating God*, *God Secrets*, *Growing Up With God*

I want to highly recommend to you this amazing new book *Prophets Among Us* by my good friend Ivan Roman. I've known Ivan for years and he has an incredible ability to communicate and articulate Kingdom truths as a prophetic teacher. Not only is Ivan a revelator but he moves in the miraculous as part of the emerging Elijah Company coming forward in this season. We have entered into a new prophetic era and a new eagle is emerging that will take us higher than we've ever been before. Its crucial that we understand our place in the Kingdom of God and timing in human history in order to fulfill our mandate. The book you hold in your hand contains the keys to unlock your gifts and reveal your identity that will in turn propel you into your destiny. This book will change your life.

Jeff Jansen, Co Founder of Global Fire Ministries International, Global Fire Center & Church, Author of *Glory Rising*, *Furious Sound of Glory*

In *Prophets Among Us*, Ivan Roman hits it out of the park. He delivers a complex subject just the way you'd want it. With personal story after personal story, Ivan brings out how God chased him down with the supernatural; an unseen hand pulling him back just in time for the bullet to miss his head. In the same way, God is *after you* because he wants to *talk* and have *relationship* with you. You're going to love the "fireside chat" style as Ivan weaves great illustrations and stories together to teach in an easy-to-understand way all about how modern-day prophets and prophecy operate This is a complete work. There are no missing subjects. Get yourself a copy and buy one for a friend while you're at it!

Steve Shultz, Founder, The Elijah List

One of the great joys in my life is knowing Ivan Roman. I have found in Ivan a man who is a treasure and falls under many headings in our relationship— friend, co-laborer, theologian and prophet. It is from this wealth of gifting that Ivan draws the text for his latest book, *Prophets Among Us*. I love how Ivan can weave a story from his life into the fabric of a complex subject like prophetic ministry and have the reader go away having captured a deeper understanding of truth and the heart of God. Ivan does this in the pulpit, in coffee shops or with a stranger in a casual conversation on the street. I love this man, this friend, and co-laborer with me in God's Kingdom. I know you will come to love him also as you are exposed to his life and ministry.

Garris Elkins, Speaker, Mentor, and Author of *The Prophetic Voice*

CONTENTS

CHAPTER ONE

"My Journey"

"But Moses said to him, "Are you jealous for my sake? Would that all the Lord's people were prophets, that the Lord would put His Spirit upon them!" Numbers 11:29.

Moses, as the leader of the nation of Israel, would sit while people came to him to inquire of God or to have him judge over disputes. He did this day and night. Moses' father-in-law, Jethro, saw how Moses was leading the nation and said in Exodus chapter 18, "The thing that you are doing is not good. You will surely wear out, both yourself and these people who are with you, for the task is too heavy for you; you cannot do it alone." Jethro helped Moses create a strategy so that Moses wouldn't have to judge the whole nation by himself. This was a good plan. God had a better one.

In Numbers 11:16, The Lord told Moses, "Gather for Me seventy men from the elders of Israel, whom you know to be the elders of the people and their officers and bring them to the tent of meeting, and let them take their stand there with you." God was giving Moses a support team to help him bear the burden. Moses chose his 70 and called them to the tent where God ministered to them and they all prophesied. Two of the men Moses chose, however, Eldad and Medad, stayed home. And even though they didn't attend the tent meeting, they too began to prophesy. Joshua, Moses' assistant, ran over to Moses and complained. "Moses, these two guys didn't come to the *conference*. They didn't *pay*. They didn't get *ordained* or *commissioned*, and yet they're prophesying." Moses' response was Numbers 11:29, "Are you jealous my sake?" Remember Moses was functioning as the prophet for a nation and was burning out. The cry of Moses' heart reflected the same cry of God's heart; "I wish that all God's people were prophets and that He would put His Spirit upon all of them!"

We see this prayer fulfilled in Acts 2 when the Spirit of God was poured out and the believers began to prophesy. Now, the Spirit of prophecy isn't for the few but for all who receive the Spirit. In one sense, we are all prophets because we are all called to hear the voice of God, to obey his voice, and to share what he says. Look deeper into the bible, though, and it also says we are *not* all prophets.

Radically Saved

Through my journey with the Lord, I feel like I stumbled upon the prophetic call. I didn't grow up as a Christian. I didn't have Angelic encounters as a child proclaiming I was a prophet. We hear testimonies from people who were called by God in powerful ways; visited by an angel; the audible voice of God. We naturally assume, if it didn't happen to us, we can't be prophets. We wrestle with Jesus' call for our lives. For me, nothing happened until I was radically saved.

I was nearly shot in a drive by shooting. I was in Philadelphia, pass-out drunk, leaning on a post on the side of the road when the shooting happened. I felt someone grab me by the back of the shirt and yank me backward. I felt the bullet whiz past me and hit a man nearby, striking him in the hip. My life was literally saved. Right after that, the still, small voice of the Lord asked me, "Where would you go if you died right now?" I said, "Well, I'm really drunk. I guess I would go to hell." He asked another question. "Where was that man shot?" Suddenly I saw myself in a vision, leaning against the post. The bullet rushed straight toward my head but something intervened and pulled me out of the way, causing the bullet to miss my head.

Afterward, I began searching for the one who saved me. My uncle invited me to his church, one of those really weird churches that believed in the move of the

Holy Spirit. People were shaking under the power of God. Some were laughing. Others appeared to be taking naps in the hallway, though they were actually resting under the power of the Spirit. I thought, *What in the world is this?* Having come from a Catholic background, I had never seen anything like it. However, I felt the same presence that saved me was also there, and so I gave my life to Jesus. Right after, my uncle, said "Here's what you need to do. You need to go home, get on your knees and ask Jesus to fill you with the Holy Ghost." I didn't know anything about this "Holy Ghost" but I knew I was supposed to ask Jesus to fill me. I knelt down by my bed and said, "Jesus, fill me with the-" Before I could even finish the question, I was speaking in tongues. I had no idea what was going on. From then on, I started having supernatural experiences, but I had no grid as to what was normal for a Christian. I thought all the experiences I was having were normal.

I remember at one service, I was worshiping with my eyes closed when I saw a picture of this super narrow hallway. Clearly, at the end of the hallway, I saw this throne but all the way along the hallway were doors. I knew these doors were distractions, and I knew that if I went through any, it would keep me from my goal which was the King sitting on the throne. I came out of this experience and went to speak to my uncle. I told him, "Jesus wants me to walk a narrow path." He said, "Yeah! Of course. That's a verse in the bible." I had never read the bible. God continued to speak to me through visions and dreams.

In one dream I had in those early days, one of my family members was pregnant. This particular family member, though, wasn't able to have children. I figured the dream got it wrong so I called a different family member and asked if she was pregnant, to which she replied, "No honey, I'm not." I learned later that the family member who couldn't conceive, the very same one from the dream, was in fact pregnant.

I was 20 years old, I had just been radically saved, but didn't feel that my church had much to offer someone my age. As so often happens, I started to fall away, back into my old ways of living. I couldn't understand the purpose of church at that time. Then I had a supernatural wake-up call of a sort. This was before I had any teaching on the prophetic or knew I was called to be a prophet. A demonic spirit entered my bedroom. The best way to describe it is that the darkness became darker than the dark. The lights were on but I couldn't see a thing. I became aware of a demonic spirit in the room. It felt like a spirit of torment and fear. I curled up into a ball and cried. I had a thought that I didn't want to wake my parents who at the time weren't saved. All of the sudden, deep on the inside of me, I heard, "The blood of Jesus. The blood of Jesus." I began to echo the voice and I shouted "The blood of Jesus! The blood of Jesus!" It was a New Jersey winter's night so I had the windows closed, but from somewhere wind blew loudly into my room. It blew directly over my chest and peace came over me. I heard my name spoken into my right ear, "Ivan!" I heard it audibly. Then, I fall asleep.

The next morning I woke up and immediately thought about the experience. The voice I heard couldn't have been my dad. He has a very distinctive voice, like a Puerto Rican Godfather. I started pacing back and forth, mulling it over. Eventually, I realized the voice had to be God. At that realization, I lost it and started to cry. I was confused. I thought about Charlton Heston as Moses and the voice of God in that movie. It was loud and booming. "Moses!" But when God said my name, there was no boom. He didn't give me any direction or input. He just called out my name and nothing more. I asked him, "Why didn't you speak to me?" Then I heard a voice way down on the inside say, "Because I'm calling you. Whenever you are ready to follow me, I'm calling you." This was the beginning of my Christian experience. When I shared these experiences with other believers they said, "No, God doesn't speak like that anymore." "No no no, how long have you been saved? There's no way you've only been saved for three weeks and you're already having visions." I stopped talking about my prophetic experiences with people. It seemed to make them jealous or angry.

My First Mentor

That changed when I attended a conference in the year 2000 whose guest speaker was a man named Todd Bentley. The venue was a church where, on Sunday mornings, you wore a suit and tie and then in the evening, you took the tie off but left on the sports coat. Here came Todd wearing a T-shirt, sports coat, ripped jeans, the back of his underwear hanging out, a chain wallet, drinking a Starbucks and coca-cola in a sanctuary where the only liquid allowed was holy water. I was so offended by this guy. I was offended by the way he spoke. I was offended by the way he prayed for people. He didn't gently ask for the Holy Spirit to come. He shouted "BAM!" and people fell over. Then, he operated in word of knowledge and I had never seen anything like it before. He called people out by name and by address. He would say "Sir, in the back, I had a vision of a yellow pick-up truck, and it was going through a four-way stop and it was hit on the side." The man would respond, "Yeah!" Then Todd would say, "Your L5 was injured," and the power of God would heal the man.

You see, I had my own experiences with the Lord and I believed those, but I had a hard time believing in anyone else's experiences. I had seen Christian television with people who had the big hair and the blue eye makeup, and I thought Todd was just like those guys. Probably had a little microphone in his ear with someone feeding him information. I remember checking out the inside of his ear from where I sat. I thought, *There is no possible way he could know this kind of information about someone's life.*

He walked up to my aunt Doris who was like a second mom to me. I'm Hispanic, and in the neighborhood where I grew up, in that culture, your mom can spank you, your grandma can spank you, your aunt can spank you, and your neighbor can spank you. Even your neighbor's aunt can spank you. Family and community are a big part of your upbringing. When Todd ministered to my aunt, I already knew she had a degenerative knee condition. Todd stood in front of her and read her mail. He then spoke details about my brother who wasn't in the room. He was at camp Pendleton in the Marine Corp. I slowly sank down into my chair and looked the other way. I prayed this guy wouldn't prophesy over me. Meanwhile, Todd prayed for my aunt and she got healed! She started doing things she hadn't been able to for a long time. I was just thinking, *No! This just like that weird stuff on TV.* However, the power of God was so present and so evident, I knew it was real and I knew it was what I was longing for. It was amazing how religious I'd become in only six months since being saved. Matthew 16:6 says "Beware of the leaven of the Pharisees."

That night, I went home, laid on my face and said, "Jesus, if you could use me as you use this man, have him invite me to travel with him." The next day, during the service, Todd pointed to me in the crowd of 500 and said, "Young man, if you have a desire to travel with me, I extend an invitation to you." He prayed for me and then prophesied over me, calling me out as an evangelist," (more about that later). I traveled all over the world with Todd. Under the ministry of an evangelist, I saw the deaf hear, the lame walk, and the blind see. I saw a woman whose eyes were white with cataracts. As we prayed for her, she was crying and being touched by the Spirit of God. As she cried, her tears washed the cataracts away and I could see her pupils. We saw the power of God. People were delivered of demons and I saw many signs and wonders.

In my travels with Todd, I realized I had a heart for the lost. I was moving under the umbrella of an evangelist but my DNA seemed extremely different. I tended to want to be alone. I was more of an intercessor, more contemplative. I was soaking all the time so that I could hear the voice of God. Todd would pray for someone and boom! They were on the ground and healed, or got up out of their wheelchair. That wasn't necessarily happening to me. When I prayed for somebody, I would weep with compassion, at which point I would begin to see pictures. I could easily discern what was going on.

A Seer Anointing

Once, on a trip, a youth pastor asked me to share my testimony. It was my first time sharing it publicly and I was incredibly nervous. When I finished, I didn't know what else to say or do. The youth pastor said, "Pray for the kids."

"What do you want me to pray about?" I asked.

"Let me show you," he said. "Close your eyes and ask Jesus to speak to you. Whatever he gives you to say will bless the kids." I closed my eyes and began to receive revelation from the Holy Spirit. I had seen people operate in the revelatory realm but this early in my journey, I hadn't yet prophesied over anybody. I laid hands on the first person and saw all this information about their life. I prayed, and when I looked up, they were crying. The youth pastor was crying, too. He looked at me and said, "Good job, good job!" I went onto the next one. I prayed and the same thing happened. I saw the picture, got the download, prayed it over them, and they'd cry.

But I held something back. Earlier that day I had a vision in the spirit. I saw a little girl get hit by a car. I saw as she got thrown and hit her head. In the vision, I saw her head repeatedly hit the pavement. I didn't want to share it because it was a small youth group. After the meeting, I got in the car with the youth pastor and he told me what a great job I had done and that he was proud of me. He was so fatherly, I felt free to share with him the vision I'd received. I said I wasn't sure if it was the Lord, that I was still learning. He said, "She was there at the meeting but she had to leave because of a headache from the car accident." From then on, the prophetic operated in me. It wasn't just in random dreams and visions that the Lord spoke to me but in a new and more constant flow.

After that trip, we went to a conference in Alaska. I sat in the back, interceding and praying in tongues. All of the sudden my eyes were open and I saw with open eyes into the realm of the spirit. I saw words written over people. I saw colors over their heads. I saw open visions over people. I walked over to some of them to tell them what I was seeing. Some responded with, "That was a dream I had." I would then explain their dream through the lens of the vision. I told one woman I saw the words "medical missionary" written above her head. She became emotional and told me she used to be in medical missions but left it behind when she had a family. She confessed it was still a deep desire in her heart.

As this happened more and more, my mentor and the mentors around me started telling me that I was a seer. "Wait a minute. I thought I was an evangelist?"

They would say, "Well, I think that we may have missed it. You are evangelistic and you have a heart for the lost. You can come under and function as an evangelist. But your anointing is as a seer."

I began to be invited to these meetings called presbyteries. I had only been saved for 6 months, and I was sitting in a prophetic presbytery with pastors and leaders. I'd be sitting there, someone would walk into the room, and I would go into an open vision. The problem was that I had no interpretation. I would just tell everything that I saw. Fortunately, my mentors usually had the interpretation because I had not developed that gift.

At that point in my journey, people, even the leaders who I was closest to and knew me well, started identifying me as 'the prophetic guy."

Identifying Your Calling

You may discover or have already discovered, that those who know you really well, like your parents, your best friends, or your spouse, can identify your calling. Others may try and fail, or they'll try and only give you a piece of the larger picture. What happened to me was that, whatever season of life I was in, that was the prophetic word spoken over me. I was at a conference and somebody said, "I see power evangelism all over you." I thought, *Okay, power evangelism. Evangelism with signs and wonders. I'm kind of doing that already.*

At another conference, the speaker said, "Sir, stand up! I see an apostolic mantle on your life." I thought, *Whoa! First, I'm an evangelist. Then my mentors said I'm a seer prophet, and now this guy is saying that I am an apostle. Good night!* Another time, this well-known prophet was speaking and I must have been tired because I nodded off. At one point, my friends shook me and told me to pay attention because the prophet was about to do an impartation.

When I went forward to receive, he stood in front of me and said, "Teacher!" I laughed to myself, thinking he had missed it. But then he laid hands on me and the spirit of God hit me. I went flying backward three rows. I was on the ground thinking, *I'm a Teacher. Wow! How can one person be everything?*

Sometime later, I was at a church standing behind a pastor. He paused, turned around, looked down at me very dramatically, and said, "I feel like the Lord told me to give you my mantle." *Uh oh!* He took off his necklace and put it around my neck. I thought, *What the heck? I'm traveling with an evangelist and now I have the mantle of a pastor. Do I need to leave and go to seminary? Do I need to now learn how to be a pastor?*

What I realized during that season was I was trying to find my identity in a title, not in who I was in Christ. None of those prophetic words helped to define my calling; they only brought more confusion and frustration. I can tell you right now, I am not all of the five-fold ministries. During that season of my life, God had to adjust my mind and heart so I would no longer find my identity in a title. I had no clue who I was and I was looking for someone to tell me. I felt like a kid walking around asking "Are you my mommy? Are you my daddy?" I asking "Please, somebody, tell me who I am!" I started to burn out from all the confusion.

A Hat for Ivan

One time, I found myself thrown in with eight young apostolic prophetic leaders in Kansas City. I had no idea what I was doing there. By this time, I was totally burned out. On a whim, I went to a nearby bookstore with a friend. I said to my friend, "Check out this book. It was written just for me." It was a Max Lucado children's book called *A Hat For Ivan*. I told my friend, "The Lord is going to speak to me through this book." I was just kidding. Then I opened the book and read. It was about a kid from Hatville whose father was the hat-maker. At the age of ten, everybody in Hatville was given a hat that suited them perfectly. When it was Ivan's turn, he went around town as usual but this time every person he met gave him a hat. Not a single one fit. I started to cry openly in the bookstore. At the end, Ivan ran into his father and told him about his day, about all the hats, how none of them fit, and how tired it made him to carry them all around.

"Listen, son, just because someone gives you a hat, that doesn't mean you are supposed to wear it. They mean well, but they don't know you. That's my job. I'm the hat-maker, and I'm your father… What do you really love to do?"

I got so rocked by the Holy Spirit in that moment. From then on, I said "I don't care if I'm this, or that, or anything. I just want to walk in intimate friendship with Jesus." I started hearing testimonies that also rocked my life; testimonies of men like Paul Cain, a well known prophet, where he and Mike Bickle, leader of the International House of Prayer, were in a restaurant having dinner. As their meals arrived, Paul asked if they could move to a quieter corner of the dining floor. The runner who brought their food was happy to oblige but asked, "Don't you think your waitress is going to be a little annoyed with you?" Once they'd moved, Mike was so frustrated with Paul he couldn't keep quiet.

He said, "I'm wrestling with why you wanted to be moved. Is there a reason?"

Paul said, "Well, our waitress has kidney stones, and every time she comes to fill my glass my kidneys start to hurt. That couple over there are having a bad time in their marriage, and that young kid over there is having a rough time in his life." Paul had discerned what was happening all the way around the restaurant, which is why he wanted to be in the corner away from everyone.

Mike then said as their waitress went past, "Excuse me, but do you have kidney stones?"

"How'd you know?" she asked.

Mike said to Paul, "We could have revival right now. Just start calling out everything you see."

Paul put his head down and said, "You may not understand this, but a long, long time ago Jesus came to me and said 'Paul, I call you my friend, and I am going to share secrets with you, and these secrets aren't for you to tell everybody. I just want you to know what is on my heart.'"

When I heard this story, it blew my mind. My ministry had been all about the gifts that operated through me. I had been trying to find my identity in a gifting. Now I was hearing stories where the gifting isn't what was important; it was friendship. I could have a friendship with Jesus and hear his voice that way.

Another one of my favorite stories is about the late seer prophet, Bob Jones, told to me by an associate pastor at a church where Bob was ministering. He was probably in his late 70s at this time. He said in his thick Arkansas accent, "Yip, I've been here before."

The pastors said, "Oh no, Bob. You've never been here before. This is the first time you've been here, and we are so honored to have you."

Bob replied, "Nope! I've been here before."

"No, sir. I've been the pastor here for about 15 years. I'm pretty sure you've never been here."

"Boy! Don't you tell me where I've been and haven't been before. Take me around the building." The pastor took him on a tour of the church, and Bob said, "Yip, y'all painted the building three months ago." Sure enough, it had been exactly three months to the day that they'd painting the church.

The pastor said, "How did you know?"

Bob said simply, "I told you I'd been here before. My friend always takes me places before I go."

After hearing this story I thought, *translating in the spirit is pretty cool.* But what stood out most to me was that this was something God did out of relationship with his friend.

A Friend of God

I started to feel used by God. Have you ever prayed, "God use me!" and then wonder why you felt used? I wanted to walk in friendship with God instead. I wanted to hear his voice out of intimacy and relationship instead of just gifting. I came to a place in my ministry where I couldn't give a rip about titles or gifting. All I wanted was to pursue intimacy with Jesus. During that season, my gifting actually grew because faith works through love.

I hosted another event in Alaska. The preacher was from Staten Island, New York and had this really fun, rich accent. At one point he said, "The Lawd's releasin' mantles." I closed my eyes and went into the spirit. Right away I saw this brown mantle in my mind and I asked the Lord what He was showing me. As the mantle descended, I went into an open vision and I saw the Lord Jesus standing in front of me. I didn't see his face but I knew it was Jesus. I heard him say, "Today, I call you my friend, and I will make you a recognized prophet to your generation." As I heard this, I recognized that Jesus emphasized certain things, "*Today* I call you my friend, and I will *make* you a recognized prophet to *your* generation." The significance of the encounter was so strong, I fell on my face. From the floor, I heard the worship team prophesy about being friends of God. My friend Amy Ward was there and she also heard the Lord call her a friend. It was a word that redefined many who heard it, and many of us have gone to pioneer new movements. It all started when God called us his friend.

After that, I began to have experiences while brushing my teeth or doing my hair or using the restroom. Visions would flash in front of me, all while doing menial everyday tasks. I saw things that weren't always beautiful or something I could write in an article, or stand in front of people and speak about. Once, I woke in the middle of the night to pray for a president, and later that day learned the president had been assaulted but saved. I became this undercover friend with Jesus.

Some prophetic people want to share every single thing the Lord tells them but this comes from a place of immaturity or being young in the gift. As you grow in your friendship with God, you understand that God wants to be able to trust you with secrets. Not everything he shares with you is to be shared with others.

The Five-fold Ministry and the Gifts of the Spirit

The title of prophet doesn't matter nearly as much as the function. Ephesians 4:11-12 says the purpose of the five fold ministry is that "He gave some to be apostles, and some as prophets, and some as evangelists, and some as pastors and teachers for the equipping of the saints for the work of service to the building up of the body of Christ." The five fold ministry is for the equipping of the saints.

I've heard some say, "Because I'm in Christ, I have all the gifts of the spirit. I have all the five fold." I want to address this belief.

If you're born-again, you're filled with the Holy Spirit. You are a new creation. Your sins, past, present, and future, are forgiven. You are the righteousness of God in Christ Jesus. You have become a partaker of His divine nature. The same spirit that raised Jesus from the dead lives in you. The Spirit of God lives in you and makes his home in you, and the gifts of the Spirit and the manifestations of the gifts of the Spirit point to the fact that Jesus rose from the dead. First, the gifts testify to the resurrection of Jesus. Second, they testify that Christ lives in you.

There is no way to have supernatural revelation about somebody else if the Holy Spirit doesn't live within you.

Because Jesus lives in you, does that necessarily imply you have all of the five fold?

1 Corinthians 12:28-30 says, "And God has appointed in the church, first apostles, second prophets, third teachers, then miracles, then gifts of healing, helps, administrations, various kinds of tongues. All are not apostles, are they? All are not prophets, are they? All are not teachers, are they? All are not workers of miracles, are they? All do not have gifts of healings, do they? All do not speak in tongues, do they? All do not interpret, do they?"

What Paul is driving at is "No!" Not all are apostles, not all are prophets. But we charismatic believers say, "Wait a minute. Of course we can all speak in tongues. Of course we can all heal the sick." What then is the context of these scriptures?

Romans 12 lists for us the seven motivational gifts of the Spirit. I hold to the belief that every single believer has one of these motivational gifts, whether it's prophecy, serving, giving, leading, showing mercy, teaching, or exhortation. Basically, it's the original Myers-Briggs test of the Bible. It's the gift that motivates you. The mercy giver, for example, maybe has more than one cat, or they may invite the homeless into their home. Even the unsaved have these tendencies in their DNA, a natural propensity towards one or another gift because of how God created them, waiting to be fully unlocked after salvation.

The Romans 12 prophet is both the motivation for how they view the world and part of their personality. Some unsaved people may still operate in a shadow of their prophetic gifting. They might call it intuition. It's how God wired them. It isn't a demon or a spirit of divination. They were created in such a way that they lean toward the supernatural. These people, if they don't encounter Jesus, often end up in the occult or in the New Age movement. But it doesn't start there.

I remember when I was about 18 I told my mom that I was going out with my friends. She said, "I really feel like you should stay home tonight." Typical overprotective mom, right? But I had my big boy pants on so I left anyway. That night, when hanging out with my friends, one of the most horrendous accidents I've ever seen happened in our immediate vicinity. Some underage guys were racing while drunk and crashed. It was a devastating accident. Ambulances were sounding off. They sent in helicopters. All of this within earshot of my home and my mother You can just imagine my mom's worry for me. She had discerned something was going to happen. You might call it a mother's intuition or it could have been someone operating out of a Romans 12 motivational gift of a prophet.

Then we have the 1 Corinthians 12 gifts of the Holy Spirit. These gifts have two camps of belief. The Pentecostal understanding is that the gifts are *resident*. In other words, you have one gift. If you walk past a sick person, and you have the gift of prophecy, you would call your pastor who has the gift of healing to pray for them. The Charismatic understanding is that the Holy Spirit gives gifts as he wills and that the gifts are *transient*. Again, if you have the gift of prophecy and walk past someone in need of healing, you can lay hands and the gift of healing would come upon you to heal the person. In that way, you have access to all the gifts of the Holy Spirit but operate primarily out of one.

Coming back to the five-fold giftings in Ephesians 4, these are known as the ascension gifts. Some who realize they can operate in the prophetic think that they must, therefore, be a prophet. Well, maybe not. You may just be operating in it as a believer, the gift being transient and given to you as the Spirit moves, not as an office-holder. The gift of prophecy and the office of the prophet can both be extremely accurate. Three differences between the two, however, are platform, favor, and influence.

A lot of people say, "I had that word, too, before it was ever posted on the Internet by that well-known prophet." That may be but you didn't have the same influence. That's not to say larger ministries weren't small at some point in their past. Everybody starts somewhere. But office prophets are often propelled into world-changing situations.

There's a prophet by the name Kim Clement. I remember the first time I saw him minister. I wasn't familiar with him, and I have to be honest, it wasn't really

14

my style. He took the stage, his long hair bouncing as he bobbed his head shouting Hebrew words of praise. I'm Puerto Rican and from New Jersey. In my flesh, I have to admit, I was judging the man. But then he began to minister, and he just read people's mail! In super accurate detail! I thought, *Oh Lord! Forgive me! It might not be the package or wineskin that I'm used to, but boy, this guy hears God!*

The thing about Kim Clement is, he's got platform, favor, and influence. He had a word back in 2004 about a "burning bush" burning brightly in the white house, a word for and about President Bush. Kim was able to get that word into the hands of the president himself. That's an office prophet.

It's the same with Bobby Conner, a respected prophet, and Bob Jones. The first time he met Bob, Bobby had a dream the night before about a woman in a green dress assassinating President Clinton. Later, as he picked up Bob Jones in his car for a meeting that night, Bob asked him what the Lord was showing him. "We're just excited to have you at this meeting," exclaimed Bobby.

Bob Jones: "Not about that, boy! About the woman in the green dress!"

Together, somehow, Bob and Bobby got word to the president to avoid a potential tragedy. Bobby's actual words to me were, "We got it to him."

All believers are called to be ministers of the gospel but few actually make their living from it. Equippers are those called to equip the Bride and enter full-time ministry to the church. In North America, the idea of earning a living as a minister can be attractive, especially in rock star-Christian culture. But that's not a biblical model. The biblical model is that the equipper prepares those around her with the grace that is on her life.

What are some ways to know if you are walking as a prophet and not just in the gift of prophecy? If I walk into your house when you have the chickenpox, but you say you have the measles, do I walk out with what you say you have or with what you actually have? What is the impartation of your life and what is the fruit of your ministry?

"Not all are apostles, not all are prophets, not all are teachers." You could be a Romans 12 motivational teacher but not be an Ephesians 4 equipping teacher.

The 1 Corinthians 12 gifts, additionally, are the public ministry gifts. "Not all work miracles." However, in Mark 16 we read, "You shall lay hands on the sick and you shall see them recover." When we pray in Jesus' name, there is power whether you have a gift of healing or not. Whether or not you've ever seen anybody healed, you can lay hands on the sick and see them recover because we call on the name above any other name. Every knee will bow, every tongue will confess, every sickness and every disease must submit to Jesus' name. There are those who according to 1 Corinthians 12 have gifts of healing. They experience greater success when praying for the sick. Notice that the scripture says gifts with an "s," not gift. Some may have an anointing to see backs healed but may not have success with deaf ears. There are *gifts*, plural, of healing. There are those that have such a solid healing gift that they become a specialist according to 1 Corinthians 12:28. They travel to different ministries, they preach, and they pray for the sick. It's what they do.

"All do not speak with tongues, do they? All do not interpret." Remember, these are the public ministry gifts. We do not see this gift of tongues often anymore but we use to see it all the time. There was a time you could go to a Pentecostal church and see someone stand and shout in tongues. As soon as they'd sit, someone else would stand and give the interpretation in King James vernacular. Unfortunately, it proved an unhealthy example because the interpretation often didn't align with God's word or God's nature. Nowadays, if someone starts shouting in tongues during a service, the pastor waves to the worship team to get louder.

Understand that 1 Corinthians 12:28 talks about public ministry specialists. You can heal the sick, yes, and you can prophesy according to 1 Corinthians 14:39, "Desire earnestly to prophesy," but it doesn't necessarily mean you are an equipper.

Calling Up the Younger Generation

How could I receive a prophetic word that I was an evangelist, and then after a short time, receive another word be that I was a seer? Acts 13:1 says, "Now there was at Antioch, in the church that was there, prophets and teachers: Barnabas, and Simeon who was called Niger, and Lucius of Cyrene, and Manaen who had been brought up with Herod the tetrarch, and Saul." These men were called prophets and teachers but were also sent out as apostles. One theological perspective is that you graduate up the ladder of ministry to apostle. The second perspective, the one I believe, is that there are fresh assignments and fresh commissioning. They were prophets and teachers, yes, but a fresh anointing rested upon them and they were recommissioned as apostles to the body of Christ. It was a mantle swap. The primary gift, though, continued to reside within them. If you were functioning as a prophet, and the Spirit of the Lord launched you into the role of an apostle, it doesn't mean that you lose the prophetic gifting.

So there could have been a recommissioning, or the prophetic words could have been wrong. It's important to understand that prophetic people are still *people* who try really hard to get it right but don't always. If we encourage communities to practice the prophetic, and we should, know that sometimes people are going to get it wrong. There was a generation that pioneered the five-fold ministry but many of them taught that you couldn't become a prophet until you reached a certain age. Exactly how old do you have to be? Should you be at least 70 years old to be a prophet or an apostle? Where's that in the bible? How old was Jesus when he started his ministry? I wonder what the disciples' thoughts on this would be. If you want to know what people think, ask this question: how old do you think the disciples were? "Oh, at least 50." Nope. The disciples were around 20, or younger. Jesus was 30 and considered a rabbi when he found his disciples. They were released as apostles only after 3 ½ short years of walking with Jesus. This doesn't mean they were perfect in their character or fully mature in their call. I once heard Jack Hayford say, "Why is it the older we get, the harder we make it for the next generation?" What happens when you see 12-year-old David, just a kid, anointed and called to be king? Do we avoid telling him he's a king so it won't go to his head? The truth is, the same way an acorn possesses the DNA of an oak tree, David, when commissioned, possessed the seeds that would eventually mature and cause him to be king. Young ministers need someone to walk alongside them. They need a mentor to teach them and call them higher, especially in the realm of the prophetic.

Mentoring the next generation is vital. When you function in a fivefold capacity, you have experiences where, when you share them with other people, they think you're crazy. One of the first questions you might be asked when checked into a psychiatric hospital is "Do you hear voices?" If we went by their standards, I guess we'd all be admitted. We hear, not voices, but one voice: the voice of God. We are called to be a peculiar people. We need to be careful to not just teach Prophecy 101 over and over again. We need to actively mentor those who are called to function either in a high revelatory realm or the office of a prophet or even those just hungry so that they can stop feeling crazy.

How do you come alongside and teach people experiencing the prophetic who have no grid for it? My son, who's 11 years old, has the calling of a prophet on his life. One night, my wife and I were praying together. I was preparing to preach that following morning and my son ran into my room and he said, "Daddy! Mommy! I saw Jesus! He walked into my room."

"That's good son," I said. "Go back to bed." I was walking in super unbelief. I thought it was cute but that he was just trying to stay up late and knew to pull the Jesus card on daddy because I get excited. But he went on to explain the vision he'd had in detail.

Then he said, "Dad, stand up!" Suddenly I felt like I was in a revival service.

"Awe, son," I said. "Daddy is in bed and I'm already in my night clothes." He started to prophesy over me anyway. He put his hand on my stomach and said, "Jesus says that your heart's way bigger than your stomach." I didn't know what to say. Then he prophesied over my wife, who began weeping as she watched her son prophesy after having an encounter with Jesus. The whole time I was struggling with unbelief. Why, when I was trying to pioneer the supernatural? Because, the older generation tends to struggle when the younger generation starts to walk in what they, the pioneers, have been contending for. I had to repent for harboring unbelief towards my boy. With my son, I don't force him to minister. I don't want to do that. However, if he's receiving things from the Lord for people, then I want to *encourage* him to minister.

I remember a ministry trip to Canada where my boy was with me. This big Native American man walked up, so tall he seemed to hover over us. I closed my eyes but my son looked deep in his eyes and he said, "You are so tired." The man burst into tears. I had no idea what was happening. My son, though, he continued to walk around and read people's mail. Later, I heard testimonies of just how accurately he prophesied. At one church, he said, "I see bullets flying through the building," and he shared his interpretation. What he didn't know was that there had been a shoot-out at the convenient store across the street and bullets had flown through the sanctuary.

I ministered at an event with Shara Chalmers Pradhan and her husband Danny. During a service, my son was at the end of a fire tunnel holding up the line because he was reading everyone's mail. That night while at home, he jumped out of bed to tell me all about it. "Dad, the fire of God came into my heart. And Jesus began speaking into my ear, and I just said everything that I heard him say." What was I supposed to tell him? "Well, son, that's great but you held up the line. You really need to work on your character." Of course not! I know character is critical but Romans 11:29 says the gifts are given without repentance. You can have a gift and not even be walking with Jesus. It says in Matthew 7:22-23, "Did we not prophesy in your name?... And then I will declare to them, I never knew you; depart from Me, you who practice lawlessness." 1 Corinthians 13:2 says, "If I have the gift of prophecy... but do not have love, I am nothing." Character is important for lasting fruit and longevity in ministry but we should encourage the spiritual gift, too. We need to practice patience, a fruit of the spirit, while mentoring the younger generation as they walk out the gifts of the spirit.

The apostle Paul wrote to the church in Corinth to tell them they were all kinds of messed up but he started his letter this way: "To the Saints of Corinth." Why? This was their identity. He went on to describe the gross sin that took place within the church. "I hear that one of you is sleeping with your father's wife." That's some Jerry Springer level drama. What Paul didn't do was to swing the pendulum the other way and demand they focus on love alone and ignore the gifts. Instead, he wrote chapter 13, a whole chapter on love. Chapter 14 then gives proper perspective; pursue love and desire the spiritual gifts, especially that you might prophesy. Why is it so hard to see that we can pursue love and the spiritual gifts at the same time? It doesn't have to be one or the other. What's so beautiful about Jesus is that you get *all* of him.

Called to be a Prophet

How do you know if you're called to be a prophet? The same way David knew; God will call you. Whether through a dream or a personal experience, or often times through the Word, God will call you. Then it will be confirmed; sometimes through another prophet and not usually in public. Initially, a lot of the prophetic words that come will be when you're all by yourself. Getting the call is easy. The hard part is the training. This is the phase where our hearts get purified to see what's really in there. It's a process designed to challenge us and we learn what to say and what not to say.

Early in my prophetic journey, I would see something on someone, invite them out for coffee, then say something like, "The Lord is showing me that you are struggling with same sex tendencies. Is that true?" Do you think that approach made them feel loved? Not really. But that's how I did it. I used to be a part of a church where I became their prophetic pit bull. They'd say, "See what you can pick up," and I'd go sniffing in the spirit for what I could call out. Whenever Ivan was in the staff meeting, you were in trouble. Leadership would sit someone down with whom there'd been issues and set me loose. "You were abandoned by your father. Your husband left you. You have an issue with men. This is what's going on in your life..." and on like that. The person would cry and the ministers would pray. Then I'd dust my hands off and think, *job well done.* That was not operating out of love.

You have to embrace the reality that God loves people. The prophetic isn't for calling out people's sin but to call people higher. If you are called to be a prophet then you had better love people.

Many struggle with the call. I never wanted anyone to put a title in front of my name. Now, when I travel, it doesn't bother me what title they put in front of my name. My identity isn't defined by my title. If God has called you as a prophet, then embrace it in humility serve the body of Christ in love. Allow the grace to flow through you and allow those around you to confirm in due season. There is no need to have business cards made with titles on them. God and the function of a prophet itself will open the doors for your grace to be received.

CHAPTER TWO

"The Purpose of a New Covenant Prophet"

Many Christians today are afraid of the word "prophet." It evokes images of Old Testament fire and brimstone prophets. What people forget or don't know is there are prophets among us walking who function in the gift without even realizing it. Or it's kept on the fringes. The role of a prophet is on spiritual gift tests taken by all sorts of denominations who don't take it too seriously. Matthew 13:57 says "a prophet is not without honor except in his hometown." I think it's absolutely true.

How great would it be if the body of Christ were able to recognize one another for who they really are? To be able to see the gifting in each other and honor it with no envy, arrogance, insecurity, or fear? During the 1960s and 70s, titles like prophet and apostle were overused. People began to mistrust. They grew hesitant to speak about their gifting or to call it out in others. Then there's the culture of Eastern Christianity where they recognize the fivefold offices with reverence. Here in the west, in my opinion, we're so laid back that we lack honor.

Honor is biblical. You don't have to have a title, but Matthew 10:41 says, "He who receives a prophet in the name of a prophet shall receive a prophet's reward; and he who receives a righteous man in the name of a righteous man shall receive a righteous man's reward."

The Purpose of a New Covenant Prophet

The way in which you recognize someone determines the measure of the reward you'll receive. If God wants you to receive a prophet's reward but you decide, "Nah, I hear God too. Who does this guy think that he is?" You might receive a reward but not all that God had for you!

So often, when people think of a prophet, they define it like in Isaiah or Jeremiah. You imagine some guy coming out dressed in camel hair and eating locusts! Sure, we've seen some those types. When we talk about the prophetic, there is this stigma wrapped around it as if a true prophet, when giving a word, should look over your head and never at your face. Or there's the Old Testament mentality in which the prophet lives in a cave and has no friends. That may be a little extreme, but we need to realize we've embraced an Old Covenant mentality concerning prophets. We need a new definition, found in the New Testament.

By now you're already familiar with Ephesians 4:11-13. "And He gave some as apostles, and some as prophets, and some as evangelists, and some as pastors and teachers, for the equipping of the saints for the work of service, to the building up of the body of Christ; until we all attain to the unity of the faith, and of the knowledge of the Son of God, to a mature man, to the measure of the stature which belongs to the fullness of Christ." Before we establish who holds what office, let's first establish our common ground identity. John 10:3-5 says, "To him the doorkeeper opens, and the sheep hear his voice, and he calls his own sheep by name and leads them out. When he puts forth all his own, he goes ahead of them, and the sheep follow him because they know his voice. A stranger they simply will not follow, but will flee from him, because they do not know the voice of strangers." That is our identity as sons and daughters of God – we are all called to hear the voice of God.

Let's get something clear. It is not the function of a New Testament prophet to tell people what they are supposed to do with their lives. It is not anointed bossiness! Exodus 20:18-19, "All the people perceived the thunder and the lightning flashes and the sound of the trumpet and the mountain smoking; and when the people saw it, they trembled and stood at a distance. Then they said to Moses, 'Speak to us yourself and we will listen; but let not God speak to us, or we will die.'" This is how an Old Testament prophet functioned. It was part of their job to tell people how to live, according to what God instructed. The Old Covenant prophet was the mediator between God and man. If you wanted to hear what God was saying, too bad! You couldn't hear him on your own. You had to hear through the words of a prophet.

I had an experience while driving a group of young men whom I was mentoring home after a ministry trip. While driving, I went into a vision. I could see the road but I also saw in the spirit. I saw a mountain in front of me and I heard God say, "If this generation doesn't come to the mountain of the Lord to hear my voice, they will put my commandments back on stone and they will try to put me back in a box." It is much easier to try and live by a set of rules and regulations than to establish a relationship with Jesus. Many people fear living under the New Covenant where the law is love because it seemingly lacks control. "Just tell me the seven steps to get closer to God!" they plead. We all know God is too big to be put in a box. Some of you may remember a Taco Bell commercial with the little Chihuahua dog in which he had a trap set up and said, "Here lizard, lizard, lizard!" To his surprise, Godzilla arrived. "Uh oh! I think I need a bigger box!" That's how it is. God isn't going to fit into any box.

There is a way, though, that you can limit the Holy One of Israel: it resides between your ears. You can limit what God can do through your own stinking thinking. Thinking itself isn't bad—it's how we think. It's critical that we are established in this present truth. We must continue to allow the Holy Spirit to expand the wineskin of our knowledge so that we can grow with what God is doing in the Kingdom.

The Lord is inviting an entire generation to hear his voice. In Exodus 19 God invites all of his people and promises them "you shall be to Me a kingdom of priests and a holy nation." If you understand covenantal language, "I will make you…" is a *royal grant covenant*. This kind of agreement is made by a greater figure, such as a king, to lesser figures, such as the king's subjects. The responsibility for seeing that the covenant is fulfilled rests solely with the greater.

The Purpose of a New Covenant Prophet

In the Abrahamic Covenant, see the way in which God interacts with Abraham. When Abraham made a mistake, God didn't kill him. But what we see in the Mosaic Covenant in Exodus 19 is that God offered a royal grant covenant to his people, and all of the sudden, things change drastically. In order to fully understand this, we have to go to Deuteronomy 5.

God told his people, "I want all of you to be my royal priesthood! I want all of you to hear my voice and be my special people!" But in Deuteronomy 5 they said, "Moses, when God spoke, it scared us! We want you to go up there and hear for us, and whatever he tells you to do, that's what we'll do." Here, the covenant changed to a kinship covenant. They moved out from under a royal grant to a covenant of blessings and curses.

Many in the church have failed to realize what Romans 10:4 means. "For Christ is the end of the law for righteousness to everyone who believes." We are no longer under the Mosaic Covenant!

That is critical to understand.

Matthew 5:17-20 says, "Do not think that I came to abolish the Law or the Prophets; I did not come to abolish but to fulfill. For truly I say to you, until heaven and earth pass away, not the smallest letter or stroke shall pass from the Law until all is accomplished. Whoever then annuls one of the least of these commandments, and teaches others to do the same, shall be called least in the kingdom of heaven; but whoever keeps and teaches them, he shall be called great in the kingdom of heaven. For I say to you that unless your righteousness surpasses that of the scribes and Pharisees, you will not enter the kingdom of heaven."

If you take that scripture literally then we are still under the law and we need to go sacrifice some animals right now! It's probably been a while since you've killed a goat. Or, we can understand what "heaven and earth" represented in that scripture. Flavius Josephus was a first-century scholar and historian who wrote about, among many other things, the Tabernacle of Moses. He wrote in his *Antiquities of the Jews*, "When Moses distinguished the tabernacle into three parts, and allowed two of them to the priests, as a place accessible and common, he denoted the land and the sea, these being of general access to all; but he set apart the third division for God, because heaven is inaccessible to men," The Tabernacle represented "heaven and earth."

Let's look at Jesus' words in Matthew 24. "Truly I say to you, this generation will not pass away until all these things take place. Heaven and earth will pass away, but My words will not pass away." By way of historical-contextual hermeneutics, we understand Matthew 24's "generation" to be exactly 40 years. And we know from history that 40 years after Jesus' resurrection, in 70 A.D., General Titus surrounded Jerusalem and destroyed the Temple along with all the documents and lineages.

One of the things the church needs to learn is to read scripture in proper historical context. When they don't, we get prophets still operating under the Mosaic covenant. Literal heaven and earth haven't passed away but the metaphorical heaven and earth Jesus spoke of has.

Romans 4:15 says, "For the Law brings about wrath, but where there is no law, there also is no violation." Interesting! The wrath of God is connected to the law! But that's not what we hear in church. Some prophets say, "God up in heaven sneezes and we get Hurricane Katrina. He just wiped out a million people." To them, God looks a lot like Thor or some other mythological god rather than the God of the Bible.

It is imperative that we go back and understand God's original intentions in Exodus 19. His desire was to have a family with whom to commune. They rejected a royal grant covenant offer and placed themselves under a kinship covenant. Then in Deuteronomy, these guys screwed up so much that when Moses died, they moved to an even lesser covenant called the suzerain-vassal covenant. Under this new covenant, there were rules. Lots of them. And they all had to be kept for God to honor his side of the deal.

Context is as important to scripture as any other method of interpretation. When prophetic people don't understand the context of scripture, they may perceive that the Holy Spirit is saying something, but instead of calling God's people to pray over the matter, they'll declare the message as an impending judgment!

Dr. Jonathan Welton writes that experience influences validation, which influences to belief, which influences to culture. What happens is that a person has a vision of a tsunami. They attempt to validate their interpretation of the vision by pulling a scripture from the Old Testament out of context. That forms a belief system that, when God is mad at you, he gives you tumors and hemorrhoids and sends tsunamis to wipe you out. That creates an unhealthy Christian culture.

Then, if you have not allowed for a fresh experience with the Lord to move your heart, anything different or "new" you hear will immediately sound heretical. In fact, your old understanding may be what's heretical. Do you have any Old Covenant mentalities that need breaking through?

Old Covenant Prophets vs New Covenant Prophets

I want to contrast an Old Covenant Prophet with a New Covenant Prophet. The Old Covenant Prophet was the Voice of God for the people.

During the times of Jeremiah and Ezekiel, they were under the Mosaic covenant. Their prophecies were along the lines of "A new covenant will I give you!" Jeremiah 31:31 says,

"'Behold, days are coming,' declares the Lord, 'when I will make a new covenant with the house of Israel and with the house of Judah.'" Ezekiel 36:26-28 says, "Moreover, I will give you a new heart and put a new spirit within you; and I will remove the heart of stone from your flesh and give you a heart of flesh. I will put My Spirit within you and cause you to walk in My statutes, and you will be careful to observe My ordinances. You will live in the land that I gave to your forefathers; so you will be My people, and I will be your God."

600 years of the Mosaic covenant and these two guys were trying to give Israel hope that something better was on its way. Why did they feel so oppressed by the covenant? The law was a tutor and a harsh taskmaster. They were freed from Egypt but in bondage to the law. However, the law pointed to Jesus! You cannot become righteous by following the law. No one can keep the law. God wanted to set his people free from it.

The Purpose of a New Covenant Prophet

Under the New Covenant, all believers have a relationship with God and can hear Him speak to them personally. The New Covenant Prophet *confirms* the Voice of God for the believer.

Romans 8:14 says, "For all who are being led by the Spirit of God, these are sons of God." If you break that down in the Greek, the word translated "led," is agó which isn't indicative of the wind just blowing you where ever. It means to be guided or led by accompaniment. Those who are personally guided and accompanied by the Holy Spirit are the children of God.

The word translated "sons of God" is *huios*. It means a son who closely resembles his father, with all rights to his father's inheritance. The Holy Spirit can guide mature children and the fruit of the Holy Spirit operates through a mature son or daughter's life. Yet we have so much fear! "Oh man, we don't want to tell people that they can be *led by the Spirit*! That leads to flaky Christians. We don't need them in our church!"

Maturity in Jesus happens when the Holy Spirit doesn't have to yell at you; he can lead you with a whisper or a glance of his eye because you are compelled by love!

Whereas the Old Covenant Prophet waited for the Spirit of the Lord to come upon him, New Covenant Prophets have God living on the inside at all times. But, this requires spiritual growth and learning to hear the voice of God.

The New Testament tells us to test prophecy. It also says words need to be confirmed by the mouths of *two or three witnesses* in 2 Corinthians 13:1.

This is seriously important! I read a commentary in which the writer believed that when the Spirit of the Lord came upon a prophet under the Old Covenant, the prophet would become totally overwhelmed by the presence of God. Often times it was accompanied by a booming voice so that it was almost impossible for them to miss the voice of God! That's why, if the prophet missed it or delivered a false word, the punishment was stoning. The Spirit of God didn't live in them; it came upon them for a moment. The first time we see the Spirit of God descend *and abide* with someone was with Jesus. It didn't just descend. It stayed.

The Purpose of a New Covenant Prophet

We New Covenant prophets, we hear the voice of God but we're permitted to miss it and live! That's why prophecy needs to be tested. People who don't realize this may say, "Well you know that person gave me a word and they missed it so they must be a false prophet." Let's tackle that issue right now.

Not a single person under the New Covenant has mastered hearing the voice of God. If you think that every time you prophesy you're 100% accurate, let me warn you with this: Matthew 16:15-23. "He said to them, 'But who do you say that I am?' Simon Peter answered, 'You are the Christ, the Son of the living God.' And Jesus said to him, 'Blessed are you, Simon Barjona, because flesh and blood did not reveal this to you, but My Father who is in heaven.'" Jesus went on to prophesy about his death, to which Peter replied, "God forbid it, Lord! This shall never happen to you!" It was only seconds ago Peter had his shining moment. Jesus "turned and said to Peter, 'Get behind Me, Satan! You are a stumbling block to Me; for you are not setting your mind on God's interests, but man's.'" Ouch.

We need to have grace, on others and ourselves as we learn to hear the voice of God and to prophesy. We can test a prophetic word without judging or throwing rocks at the person who brought it. Old Covenant Prophets spoke about judgment. New Covenant Prophets speak *mercy* and *forgiveness*.

Hebrews 12:22-24 says, "But you have come to Mount Zion and to the city of the living God, the heavenly Jerusalem, and to myriads of angels, to the general assembly and church of the firstborn who are enrolled in heaven, and to God, the Judge of all, and to the spirits of the righteous made perfect, and to Jesus, the mediator of a new covenant, and to the sprinkled blood, which speaks better than the blood of Abel." Remember, Cain killed Abel and the blood of Abel cried out. For what did it cry? Vengeance! What does the blood of Jesus cry out? Forgiveness! Mercy!

Jesus himself is the best example of a New Covenant Prophet. Luke 9:51-56 says, "When the days were approaching for His ascension, He was determined to go to Jerusalem; and He sent messengers on ahead of Him, and they went and entered a village of the Samaritans to make arrangements for Him. But they did not receive Him, because He was traveling toward Jerusalem. When His disciples James and John saw this, they said, 'Lord, do You want us to command fire to come down from heaven and consume them?' But He turned and rebuked them, and said, 'You do not know what kind of spirit you are of; for the Son of Man did not come to destroy men's lives, but to save them.' And they went on to another village."

Take notice that Jesus didn't cast the devil out of them. He didn't rebuke the demon within them. He said, "You don't know what spirit you're of." Where did these guys get the idea of calling down fire? Elijah! Jesus was saying, "Listen, boys, that's the Old Covenant spirit. That's not how we do things anymore. You don't know what spirit you are of."

It's the same message we need to broadcast throughout the prophetic movement today; we no longer operate by Old Covenant prophetic rules. But does this necessarily mean judgment is done and gone away?

What about Judgment?

When we think of judgment we may naturally think of our modern day court system. We think of somebody on trial, and boy they're going to get judged! They're in trouble! That's the western view. In some cultures, if somebody were to kill a man, judgment means the killer would be responsible to care for both his family and his victim's family. They wouldn't understand going to prison for the crime. For them, judgment, like in the Book of Judges, means *to render decision* or *to make things right*.

Let's set aside our modern view of judgment for now and get hold of the biblical definition.

John 3:17-21 in the NASB says, "For God did not send the Son into the world to judge the world, but that the world might be saved through Him. He who believes in Him is not judged; he who does not believe has been judged already, because he has not believed in the name of the only begotten Son of God. This is the judgment, that the Light has come into the world, and men loved the darkness rather than the Light, for their deeds were evil. For everyone who does evil hates the

Light, and does not come to the Light for fear that his deeds will be exposed. But he who practices the truth comes to the Light, so that his deeds may be manifested as having been wrought in God."

The NIV takes the Greek word *krinó* translated here as "judgment" and instead translates it as "condemned."

"For God did not send his Son into the world to condemn the world, but to save the world through him. Whoever believes in him is not condemned, but whoever does not believe stands condemned already because they have not believed in the name of God's one and only Son. This is the verdict: Light has come into the world, but people loved darkness instead of light because their deeds were evil. Everyone who does evil hates the light, and will not come into the light for fear that their deeds will be exposed. But whoever lives by the truth comes into the light, so that it may be seen plainly that what they have done has been done in the sight of God."

Let's look at the same passage once more, this time in the Message.

"God didn't go to all the trouble of sending his Son merely to point an accusing finger, telling the world how bad it was. He came to help, to put the world right again. Anyone who trusts in him is acquitted; anyone who refuses to trust him has long since been under the death sentence without knowing it. And why? Because of that person's failure to believe in the one-of-a-kind Son of God when introduced to him. This is the crisis we're in: God-light streamed into the world, but men and women everywhere ran for the darkness. They went for the darkness because they were not really interested in pleasing God. Everyone who makes a practice of doing evil, addicted to denial and illusion, hates God-light and won't come near it, fearing a painful exposure. But anyone working and living in truth and reality welcomes God-light so the work can be seen for the God-work it is."

He didn't send Jesus to the world to point an accusatory finger. He didn't come to condemn but to judge. In fact, Jesus came to save the world. In the context of John 3:17-19, judgment comes in the form of light. Some see the light and welcome its warmth and illumination. Others see the light and run for the darkness. God doesn't have to proclaim more judgment or condemnation on them, they're judged already by their reaction to the light.

You can see this again in the woman at the well. John 4:13-26 says, "Jesus answered and said to her, 'Everyone who drinks of this water will thirst again; but whoever drinks of the water that I will give him shall never thirst; but the water that I will give him will become in him a well of water springing up to eternal life.' … He said to her, 'Go, and call your husband and come here.' The woman answered and said, 'I have no husband.' Jesus said to her, 'You have correctly said, "I have no husband"; for you have had five husbands, and the one whom you now have is not your husband; this you have said truly.' The woman said to Him, 'Sir, I perceive that You are a prophet. Our fathers worshiped in this mountain, and you people say that in Jerusalem is the place where men ought to worship. Jesus said to her, 'Woman, believe Me, an hour is coming when neither in this mountain nor in Jerusalem will you worship the Father. You worship what you do not know; we worship what we know, for salvation is from the Jews. But an hour is coming, and now is, when the true worshipers will worship the Father in spirit and truth; for such people the Father seeks to be His worshipers. God is spirit, and those who worship Him must worship in spirit and truth.' The woman said to Him, 'I know that Messiah is coming (He who is called Christ); when that One comes, He will declare all things to us.' Jesus said to her, 'I who speak to you am He.'"

He doesn't point an accusatory finger but ministers to her instead. He prophesies over her, explains her current situation, and tells her she has a choice: stay where you are, how you are, or choose eternal life. He wasn't there to condemn but to offer a way out of the darkness.

Matthew 7:1-5 in the NASB says, "Do not judge so that you will not be judged. For in the way you judge, you will be judged; and by your standard of measure, it will be measured to you. Why do you look at the speck that is in your brother's eye, but do not notice the log that is in your own eye? Or how can you say to your brother, 'Let me take the speck out of your eye,' and behold, the log is in your own eye? You hypocrite, first take the log out of your own eye, and then you will see clearly to take the speck out of your brother's eye."

Here it is again in the message: "Don't pick on people, jump on their failures, criticize their faults— unless, of course, you want the same treatment. That critical spirit has a way of boomeranging. It's easy to see a smudge on your neighbor's face and be oblivious to the ugly sneer on your own. Do you have the nerve to say, 'Let me wash your face for you,' when your own face is distorted by contempt? It's this whole traveling road-show mentality all over again, playing a holier-than-thou part instead of just living your part. Wipe that ugly sneer off your own face, and you might be fit to offer a washcloth to your neighbor."

I love that it says "that critical spirit!" We were not called to be critical. Jesus is not judging people as a pretext to condemn them. We're not called to condemn people.

However, 1 Corinthians 11:31 in the NASB says, "But if we judged ourselves rightly, we would not be judged. But when we are judged, we are disciplined by the Lord so that we will not be condemned along with the world."

Now in the NIV: "But if we were more discerning with regard to ourselves, we would not come under such judgment. Nevertheless, when we are judged in this way by the Lord, we are being disciplined so that we will not be finally condemned with the world."

Here, the word *krinó* has the added prefix *dia* to make *diakrinó*. Dia appears in many English words: diabetes, dialogue, diagnosis, dialect, etc. It means *between* or *through*. Diakrinó, therefore, means to separate by way of judgment, or to distinguish. Do you see the difference yet?

Maybe it will be clearer in the Amplified (AMP) Bible: "But if we evaluated and judged ourselves honestly [recognizing our shortcomings and correcting our behavior], we would not be judged. But when we [fall short and] are judged by the Lord, we are disciplined [by undergoing His correction] so that we will not be condemned [to eternal punishment] along with the world."

When we are judged by God in the context of 1 Corinthians 11:31, we are separated only for the purpose of getting right with God. Similarly, the prophetic should not be used to condemn others but to call them out from sin.

Let's not gloss over the discipline, though. Hebrews 12:6-11, "For those whom the Lord loves He disciplines, and He scourges every son whom He receives. It is for discipline that you endure; God deals with you as with sons; for what son is there whom his father does not discipline? But if you are without discipline, of which all have become partakers, then you are illegitimate children and not sons. Furthermore, we had earthly fathers to discipline us, and we respected them; shall we not much rather be subject to the Father of spirits, and live? For they disciplined us for a short time as seemed best to them, but He disciplines us for our good, so that we may share His holiness. All discipline for the moment seems not to be joyful, but sorrowful; yet to those who have been trained by it, afterward it yields the peaceful fruit of righteousness."

There is a judgment, a discipline, for believers. But there's a risk in shaky translation. You may see a huge disaster on the news and say to yourself, "See? Hundreds of Christians died because God was judging them."

That's not biblical! Those that embrace darkness, they go down with it. For those of us in the light, living under the New Covenant in Christ Jesus, judgment looks like discipline.

What does discipline look like? Is it God giving you a tumor? NO! God doesn't give sickness. "The Son of God appeared for this purpose, to destroy the works of the devil," 1 John 3:8. Sickness entered creation after the fall. It's not a work of God. Therefore, he doesn't make you sick.

Acts 10:38 says, "You know of Jesus of Nazareth, how God anointed Him with the Holy Spirit and with power, and how He went about doing good and healing all who were oppressed by the devil, for God was with Him."

Under the New Covenant, I want God to judge me as a son! I've heard people gasp when they heard that. It's because they don't understand the word! I want the Father to come and remove everything that hinders love. I say "yes!" to my Father's New Covenant Judgment that causes me to love with purity!

There are scriptures people will try to use as trump cards. If you say to someone, "Let me share with you about Matthew 24. Let's look at what's different under the new covenant. Look at Isaiah 50 and see that God isn't angry with you." They might respond, "Wait a minute, brother! The Bible says that judgment first starts in the house of the Lord!" It's like they drop a microphone, exclaiming, "I'm right and you're wrong!" All they really did was quote scripture out of context.

Take a closer look at that scripture, 1 Peter 4:12-17: "Beloved, do not be surprised at the fiery ordeal among you, which comes upon you for your testing, as though some strange thing were happening to you; but to the degree that you share the sufferings of Christ, keep on rejoicing, so that also at the revelation of His glory you may rejoice with exultation. If you are reviled for the name of Christ, you are blessed, because the Spirit of glory and of God rests on you. Make sure that none of you suffers as a murderer, or thief, or evildoer, or a troublesome meddler; but if anyone suffers as a Christian, he is not to be ashamed, but is to glorify God in this name. For it is time for judgment to begin with the household of God; and if it begins with us first, what will be the outcome for those who do not obey the gospel of God? And if it is with difficulty that the righteous is saved, what will become of the godless man and the sinner? Therefore, those also who suffer according to the will of God shall entrust their souls to a faithful Creator in doing what is right."

Approaching again from a historical-contextual hermeneutic, I don't open the bible and assume everything is written directly to me. Failure to realize the original audience and context is where many interpretation problems arise. Who was the intended recipient of this passage? Was there a "suffering" still to come when Peter wrote this? Yes! Roman Emperor Nero was heavily persecuting the church; that's the context here. Peter was telling them, "You will suffer but it won't be as bad as it will be for those who do not receive the gospel." We are disciplined by the Lord so that we may not be condemned.

How do we apply the verse to our own lives? Peter saw the suffering the same way the Jewish teachers did, as discipline. Again, judgment as discipline for the believer is not wrath or punishment. Remember, God *disciplines* his *disciples*. When you break down these scriptural references, take care that you don't take a favorite scripture and throw it out there saying, "What about this one!" Well, what about it? What's the context? When was it written? What was the culture? Who was

35

the audience? If you really want to get the most out of scripture, become a Bible detective. This is where you will get understanding.

Another trump card verse someone might try to play is John 16:8: "And He, when He comes, will convict the world concerning sin and righteousness and judgment." "You see, brother, that's the job of the Holy Spirit. That's the job of the prophet. That's what I like to do! I like to convict everybody of their sins! That's my verse!" Are they maybe not getting the whole picture?

What do we see if we keep reading? "...Concerning sin, because they do not believe in Me; and concerning righteousness, because I go to the Father and you no longer see Me; and concerning judgment, because the ruler of this world has been judged."

Your response is there, but let's read it in a few more translations to shake ourselves out of how we may have been taught to read it. In The Message: "When he comes, he'll expose the error of the godless world's view of sin, righteousness, and judgment: He'll show them that their refusal to believe in me is their basic sin; that righteousness comes from above, where I am with the Father; out of their sight and control; that judgment takes place as the ruler of this godless world is brought to trial and convicted."

The sin that the Holy Spirit convicts people of, in this verse, is the sin of not believing in Jesus. Read it again, this time in the New Living Translation. "And when he comes, he will convict the world of its sin, and of God's righteousness, and of the coming judgment. The world's sin is that it refuses to believe in me. Righteousness is available because I go to the Father, and you will see me no more. Judgment will come because the ruler of this world has already been judged.

A person who uses this verse to justify prophetically calling out the sin in a person's life is doing so out of context. Does the Holy Spirit convict people of sins other than this? Of course! But this verse doesn't go there. We have to be so careful not to take scripture out of its original context to create doctrine or reinforce theology. That can lead to bad theology!

The Spirit of Prophecy

What then is the purpose of the New Covenant Prophet if not to declare God's wrath or punishment? Point people to Jesus. That's so simple, you guys! It's a testimony of Jesus. That is the spirit of prophecy.

The Lord once spoke to me, "I am bringing reformation that will produce a revolution. The reformation will be an understanding of the nature and character of God." I had a vision of many commentaries and the Lord said, "These will have to be rewritten because they got my nature wrong!"

"Gasp! But wait a minute! How could that be? These guys have been dead a long time! Surely they knew more than these young whippersnappers today!" Maybe. But maybe theology is progressive. We understand that Abraham, before he died and went to heaven, didn't know as much about Jesus as we do now. It's called progressive revelation. God reveals new aspects of his character over time. It goes "from glory to glory." Shouldn't this generation naturally walk closer to Jesus, and the next even closer, as he reveals himself?

They should, except that there is a pervasive Pentecostal theology that we must always go back to get something we've lost! There's nothing wrong with looking for keys, but not all keys are found in the past. We think, "We've got to go back to Pentecost! We've got to go back to Azusa Street!" And on and on. I don't want to go back! The Kingdom of Heaven is increasing and advancing all over the earth. People are being saved by the thousands right now as you read this book. We just don't hear about it because we're watching the news and thinking the world is getting darker.

We need a New Covenant Revolution! It won't happen until we've gotten hold of a new wineskin. In Matthew 9:17 Jesus tells his disciples, "Nor do people put new wine into old wineskins; otherwise the wineskins burst, and the wine pours out and the wineskins are ruined; but they put new wine into fresh wineskins, and both are preserved." It's about stretching. Old wineskins have stretched to their limit; they're not able to accept any new wine or revelation. But new wineskins are elastic; they can stretch to accommodate the fermentation and revelation to come.

However, old wineskins could possibly be reused if they were soaked in water and oil. They could be made like new again. It's a delicate process and can only be done very few times, if at all, depending on the wineskin.

It's important that we allow the Holy Spirit to continue to stretch us, soaking us in living water and anointing oil. This is made easier through fresh encounters with Jesus. Then, like Peter said in 2 Peter 1:12, you will be, "established in the truth which is present with you."

Then, when you hear scriptures in context and understand what the Holy Spirit is saying you won't go, "That's not God! Because I learned back in 1987…" "Hold on a second! In the King James version…" Listen! Right now on my cell phone, I have more commentaries and Bible versions than anyone in the past could have ever carried around with them. These, combined with reading in context and frequent encounters lead to fresh revelation! Not "new" necessarily, but a fresh understanding of God's word and nature.

Speaking of God's nature, we desperately need to understand the heart of God so that we can accurately represent him through the prophetic.

Exodus 17:6-7 says, "Behold, I will stand before you there on the rock at Horeb; and you shall strike the rock, and water will come out of it, that the people may drink." And Moses did so in the sight of the elders of Israel. He named the place Massah and Meribah because of the quarrel of the sons of Israel, and because they tested the Lord, saying, 'Is the Lord among us, or not?'"

Moses took the staff, hit the rock, and water came out of the rock to quench the thirst of all of the grumbling people. Problem solved, right? Except that God's people moved on from there and the whole thing happened again. They're in the wilderness, whining and complaining, not trusting God, and demanding Moses do something. Moses cried out to God who answered and said, not to strike a rock, but this time to speak to it. Numbers 20:8: "Take the rod; and you and your brother Aaron assemble the congregation and speak to the rock before their eyes, that it may yield its water. You shall thus bring forth water for them out of the rock and let the congregation and their beasts drink." It's important to note that the Hebrew word for "speak" in this passage, *dabar*, can be translated into many meanings. Some translate it as "speak to" while others believe it's more nuanced than that and here means "speak with." It's almost as if God asked Moses to speak with the rock as a person speaks to a friend. That's an important distinction.

He is told to speak with the rock but Moses was too frustrated with his people and took it out on the rock, symbolically judging it. Sound familiar? I can't tell you how many times I've heard believers complain about the "lukewarm church. They don't love God! Look at all the sin in Las Vegas! Look at all the sin in California! God's got to judge the sin! I mean if he doesn't judge what's happening in Vegas and Hollywood then he'll have to apologize to Sodom and Gomorrah! You know, I see the big one coming and California sliding right off into the Pacific! It's going to be God's judgment!" Their response to sin and what they "see" coming is founded in their theology. They could instead choose to be discerning, like in Acts chapter 11 when Agabus prophesied a coming famine. Instead of declaring it God's judgment, they took steps to prepare for it, sharing with those in the affected region so no one would suffer. What a concept!

Moses, however, didn't just hit the rock once but twice! Numbers 10:9-13 says, "So Moses took the rod from before the Lord, just as He had commanded him; and Moses and Aaron gathered the assembly before the rock. And he said to them, 'Listen now, you rebels; shall we bring forth water for you out of this rock?' Then Moses lifted up his hand and struck the rock twice with his rod; and water came forth abundantly, and the congregation and their beasts drank. But the Lord said to Moses and Aaron, 'Because you have not believed Me, to treat Me as holy in the sight of the sons of Israel, therefore you shall not bring this assembly into the land which I have given them.' Those were the waters of Meribah, because the sons of Israel contended with the Lord, and He proved Himself holy among them." God is faithful. Water came out of the rock. However, it cost Moses the Promised Land because he misrepresented the nature and character of God.

God wasn't yelling at the people. He wanted to speak with to them. We understand that the rock was a type and shadow of Christ. He wants to speak to the world: to the lost and dying. He wants to say, "I'm the light! I love you!" There is a rabbinic tradition concerning Jesus' intervention with the woman caught in adultery that when he knelt and wrote in the sand, he wrote the names of women with whom the men ready to kill the adulterer were themselves fooling around. The scripture in John chapter eight says they left one by one, starting with the old, as Jesus wrote their sins in the sand. When no one remained who would condemn the woman, Jesus said, "I do not condemn you, either. Go. From now on sin no more."

The law said to stone her. Jesus, the fulfillment of the law, extended grace. Grace isn't just unmerited favor: it is divine enablement. When he said, "Go and sin no more," Jesus empowered her no longer commit that sin. That's the power of the prophetic, also.

Revelation 19:10 says, "Then I fell at his feet to worship him. But he said to me, 'Do not do that; I am a fellow servant of yours and your brethren who hold the testimony of Jesus; worship God. For the testimony of Jesus is the spirit of prophecy.'"

What are some of the names attributed to Jesus? Redeemer. Restorer. Savior. If the spirit of prophecy is the testimony of Jesus, the spirit of prophecy should also be the spirit of redemption, of restoration, and of salvation. If you are delivering prophecies that have no redemptive quality, they're not from God! Even within the book of Revelation, he gives Jezebel time to repent.

When we prophesy, our hearts are exposed.

If our hearts are in the wrong place, we may find ourselves saying, "God! You are just too good! I would judge this person. Man, I would deal with this person!"

I will never forget a story that I heard about John Wimber. He called out this person in a meeting who had an STD. A woman came up, he laid hands on her, and she got healed. A few months later, at another meeting, he got another word of knowledge about a woman with an STD. The same woman came forward. He said, "I thought you were healed!"

She said, "I was! I got it again." She got healed again. Six months later she came forward again when he got the same word of knowledge. By that point, you or I might have kicked her out of the meeting. "I mean she is just that sloppy agape greasy grace—get that out of here!"

Wimber wasn't far away from that himself. He said, "God, I have friends dying of cancer while this gal gets healed of an STD and goes back and gets another one and you keep healing her." God said, "And I will continue to heal her until she realizes how much I love her." God is so much different than we are! I absolutely love that about him.

Is it possible that you can pick up something negative in the prophetic? Of course. But what's God's purpose for revealing it to you? Is it so that you can stand up in the room and declare, "This is what is going to happen...?" No! That's agreeing with the enemy! Instead, be an intercessor, take a stand, and say, "God! I plead mercy! I stand in the gap and say NO to this situation taking place."

I believe there are some prophetic people that pick stuff up in the second heaven and declare it as if it was the Lord. The Apostle Paul said in 2 Corinthians 12:2-4 says, "I know a man in Christ who fourteen years ago—whether in the body I do not know, or out of the body I do not know, God knows—such a man was caught up to the third heaven. And I know how such a man—whether in the body or apart from the body I do not know, God knows—was caught up into Paradise and heard inexpressible words, which a man is not permitted to speak."

Since Paul wrote about a third heaven, there must also be a first and second heaven. There are differing theologies on what exactly these three heavens are, but I hold that the first is Earth and our natural heavens, the third is where God makes his home, and the second is the realm of angels and demons. I believe there are people who, for whatever reason—maybe they have unresolved hurts in their hearts—tune into that second heaven. They hear the plans of the enemy, get up, and prophesy and declare it! At some churches, at some events, it earns applause.

I wouldn't applaud; I would cry.

If you hear the assignment of the enemy, rally prayer support, break that stinking curse, and pray for God's righteous redemption to come in.

There's a wrestling match going on. I can see people who fully embrace New Covenant prophecy wrestling those who have a different perspective or an old wineskin. As of this writing, my church is only four years old. Not long ago, people would walk in with whom we had no relationship and ask me, "Are you the pastor here?" I wanted to lie and say, "No! It's that guy over there," because I knew what was coming next. "I've got a word from the Lord for you! Thus saith the Lord, if you don't do A, B, and C, then God is going to do D, F, and G!"

As a young, impressionable pastor, I wanted whatever they were promising. All it did was place seeds of discouragement in my heart. Now, if someone comes and tries to give me a word I will stop them and say, "Hold on! I don't know you. What's your name?"

"My name isn't important."

"It matters to me. What's your name?"

"Oh. It's Fred."

"Fred, hold on before you give me this word. Fred, where do you live?" They'd get so frustrated! "Tell me about your family. Where do you celebrate Christmas?"

"What does that matter? I'm a prophet of God!"

"Wait a minute! That's not my core value. If you're not in community here, if you don't have accountability and relationship in connection with this house, then I would rather you keep that word with you and go. Have a great day!" I will not allow myself to be manipulated anymore by Old Covenant Prophetic mentality, or worse, a demon!

Now, if a word were to come from someone in relationship with the church, that's a different story. Under the New Covenant, it's not just the prophet in the company of prophets getting up and judging the land. The New Covenant Prophet is called to be a part of a community and establish relationships. You cannot be the eye of a body to which you are not attached. Under the New Covenant, when you share a word with someone, they have permission, through scripture, to test that word! A prophet who doesn't value accountability and relationships can't be trusted. Everything he says may be true, but his life doesn't exemplify the nature of God. Do you have a pastor? Do you have anyone with whom you are in covenant relationship? No? You just wander from church to church? Then I'm sorry, but what spirit are you of?

We'll visit this again later, but the most important thing for a prophetic person is to be in relationship with the body of Christ and to not try to be a superstar everywhere they go. I remember traveling to different places where I would prophesy the word of the Lord and I wouldn't know if it would happen or not. I hope it did! Sometimes confirmations would come but often they wouldn't. When you are a part of a community and you've given somebody a word you don't know has come to pass, then you might start avoiding that person. Right? You're like, "Oh my goodness, I hope I didn't miss it!" Maybe you did! And that's okay! Because you're growing. Humility is critical.

To recap a little: there is a judgment, but as we saw from scripture, judgment for the believer in the New Covenant is not being condemned to hell: it's the discipline of God, which is beautiful, and we want the Father to discipline us. According to scripture, God isn't condemning the world; in context, he rebuked his disciples and said, "What spirit are you of, trying to call down fire, you big dummies? That's not what I came here to do!"

I wish this message would get in the hands of so many prophetic people so it could align them to the heart of the Father. The purpose of the New Covenant Prophet is to speak mercy, not judgment. Mercy triumphs over judgment!

I heard prophet Larry Randolph once say, "My daddy taught me a saying; 'don't tell the church what's wrong with her; tell the church what's right with Jesus.'" I love that! Church, the Kingdom of Heaven is at hand! Yes, the enemy is trying to do some stupid stuff, but guess what? According to Colossians 2, he's been disarmed! Have you ever fought someone with no arms? According to 1 Corinthians 15:55-57, we have victory over the enemy, which means he's been defeated. He's got no arms *and* no feet! How does somebody fight with no arms and no legs? They use their teeth. The devil just runs his mouth. It's all lies but if we believe those lies, we give him authority and access. We need to advance the kingdom in power and authority, understanding our identities in Christ.

The Purpose of a New Covenant Prophet

My exhortation to prophets of the New Covenant is that you would, before delivering any word, understand the heart of the Father.

It's as simple as this: you hear a phrase in your heart telling you "Wake up." But maybe you haven't had your coffee today. You're angry. You get up and you bellow, "God says WAKE UP!" You yell it at God's people. But God didn't say it like that. I have three boys and my favorite thing is to wake my boys up every morning, "Hey, wake up boys! Wake up!" They yawn and say;

"Hey, Dad!" It's a joy. I don't scream at them, "WAKE UP!" We need to know when God is screaming and when he is whispering. If you don't know, then be quiet!

Don't share what you're getting if you don't know exactly how the Father's heart sounds behind the message. There is a shift happening in the prophetic; it's driven by love and operating from a better understanding of the New Covenant. When you give a prophetic word, it should carry the heart of the Father and point the hearer to Jesus. It should cause people to say, "I love Jesus more now because of that word."

Father, thank you so much for raising up a prophetic revolution of New Covenant Prophets who carry your heart to your people. Allow the church to see herself the way you see her so that we radically shift the way we minister in the prophetic. In Jesus' name, amen!

CHAPTER THREE

"Discovering Your Gift"

You've heard the call and you're a New Covenant Prophet. But, in the same way that not every pastor is the same, not every prophet operates the same either. It's important to spend time discovering your gift and learning how it functions.

Friends of God

Let's start with Abraham. The first time the word "prophet" appears in scripture is in connection to Abraham. You don't see any prophetic words recorded in scripture before then, but I believe Abraham establishes the foundation for what a New Covenant prophet is supposed to be. Remember, Abraham was a prophet before the Mosaic Covenant was in place. Prior to Genesis 20:6-7, the heathen prince Abimelech had taken Abraham's wife. "Then God said to him in the dream, 'Yes, I know that in the integrity of your heart you have done this, and I also kept you from sinning against Me; therefore I not let you touch her. Now therefore, restore the man's wife, for he is a prophet, and he will pray for you and you will live. But if you do not restore her, know that you shall surely die, you and all who are yours.'"

Once Abimelech returned Sarah, Abraham prayed and God healed him. The first time we meet a prophet in the Bible, there's no prophetic word, but there is a healing. Think about that. Before anything else, the prophetic is connected to healing.

James 2:23 says, "And the Scripture was fulfilled which says, 'And Abraham believed God, and it was reckoned to him as righteousness,' and he was called the friend of God." I absolutely love this! I believe Abraham established a foundation for God's heart, not just for prophets but for all believers in general. He paved a way for all of us to be friends with God, friends who share secrets, friends who loved spending time with each other.

There are four levels of friendship. First, there's the acquaintance. This is the superficial level, where conversation revolves around the weather or news, but nothing much deeper. Second, there's the casual friend. The conversation has moved on to common interests and activities. Third, there's the confidant. At this level, you discuss life goals and try to help each other reach them. You can trust the secrets of your heart to this friend.

The fourth and final level is intimate, or covenant friendship. At this level, you are committed to each other like you are with few others. Odds are you'll have only five or six of these your entire life. They're the ones you go to if you're in crisis. This is where most marriages are (or should be) established. This is the level of relationship God desires to walk in with his people.

A good test of a true prophet would be this question: "What is the deepest desire of your heart?" If their response is "I want to prophesy over people," that's not a good sign. The best answer would be something like, "I want to walk in intimate friendship with Jesus. I want to hear his heart and to know his secrets." I want to know God's favorite color if he has one! I want to know his favorite food. I want to know everything about him, the way he knows everything about me!

Once, while driving myself to speak at a conference in Roseville, California, I prayed, "You know Lord, I'm just going to be silly here for a minute. Why don't you pick where we stop to eat?" Now, I don't do that every day. I don't ask him to choose my outfit in the mornings or anything. But I was hungry and felt like having fun with my friend. I felt like the Lord said, "In the next few exits I want you to pull over." *The next few exits?* It was the middle of nowhere and I didn't see anything except truck stops. Soon I felt like the Lord say, "Pull over there."

"The Iron Skillet? Jesus is taking me to a truck stop!" I chuckled to myself and thought about how hungry I was and that I was probably not hearing right. It wasn't an audible voice or a vision, just an impression where it sounds like you are having a conversation with yourself. I sat down inside and said, "Tell me what's good here."

"We have delicious steaks."

Oh my goodness! Steak is my favorite food! And let me tell you, that steak at the Iron Skillet truck stop was one of the best steaks I'd ever had. It was huge, it was thick, and it was juicy. It made me laugh so hard that Jesus took me to lunch at a truck stop. That is the level of friendship that I want to walk in with him, where I understand his heart and we make each other laugh.

As believers, we should be the happiest people on the face of the earth. I believe that. This level of the prophetic, the Abrahamic prophet, is about understanding friendship. Friends have fun with one another. Hebrews 1:9 says about Jesus, "... Therefore God, Your God, has anointed You with the oil of gladness above Your companions." We need to get this image of Jesus into our heads. Psalm 2:4 says, "He who sits in the heavens laughs."

One time, I was in prayer, trying to be a *Holy Man of God*. We get this idea that, if you're in the ministry, you've got to be serious otherwise people will judge you and reject you. While praying, I had this vision in which I saw myself seated at a banquet table and the Lord Jesus is seated on the other side. But I also see all of this demonic activity on the outside and it's distracting me from Jesus. It took everything within me just to lift my head and keep the focus on him. It was like a heaviness or a depression that I knew I had to press through. When I finally looked up, Jesus was laughing. I mean gut-laughter. You know when you laugh so hard no sound comes out and you're almost wheezing? It was that! Then I started to laugh, too. As we're laughing, I can hear his voice in my head; "Look around you." The demons were gone! What's more, the banquet table had been set before me. I learned that as long as I kept my eyes on Jesus, the distractions couldn't touch me. It was like they came up against an invisible bubble, Boom! They couldn't touch me and it became hilarious!

Discovering Your Gift

I believe Jesus is inviting us, especially within the prophetic community, to laugh and to walk in joy! He wants to reveal in us the same Jesus who walked around with fishermen and tax collectors. These were the low-class guys in society. Sinners also loved hanging around Jesus. I'm sure every once in a while they probably cussed. That's one way to know if you have a religious spirit: do sinners like to be around you? Not because you're in compromise, but because you have a magnetic personality. When they get around you they say, "Man, what is it about you that when I'm around you I just feel loved? I don't feel condemned. You're always so happy!"

In Hebrew, the word *shama* means to "hear and obey." In the Old Testament when God would say, "Hear my word, O Israel!" The implication was that you would both hear and obey the voice of God. That's the heart of a truly prophetic person: "I want to hear your voice and I want to obey."

1 Kings 3:5 says, "In Gibeon the Lord appeared to Solomon in a dream at night; and God said, 'Ask what you wish Me to give you.'" Then in verse nine, "So give Your servant an understanding heart to judge Your people to discern between good and evil. For who is able to judge this great people of Yours?"

What's interesting in scripture is this phrase "understanding heart" can actually be translated as "hearing heart" because "understanding" also comes from *shama*. Solomon is asking for a heart to hear the voice of God so that he can govern the people correctly. That is what made him a great king! Not his earthly wisdom; we know where that got him in the book of Ecclesiastes. "Vanity of vanities! All is vanity." What made him a good king was the fact that he wanted an understanding heart that heard and obeyed God. He didn't rely on any other voice but the voice of the Father. We need to learn how to rely on the voice of the Holy Spirit, to say, "Father, I have no clue what to say right now. I'm going to tap into your mind and your heart."

That makes a good leader! If you're a leader and you think you have all the answers, I'm hesitant of you. If you're not praying and asking the Father for what he wants to say to people, I'm leery. I want leaders whose hearts are inclined to hear the voice of God.

The Next Level

Another type of prophet you see in scripture is Moses. What I love about Moses, once again, is that you continue to see that theme of friendship with God. Deuteronomy 34:10-12 says, "Since that time no prophet has risen in Israel like Moses, whom the Lord knew face to face, for all the signs and wonders which the Lord sent him to perform in the land of Egypt against Pharaoh, all his servants, and all his land, and for all the mighty power and for all the great terror which Moses performed in the sight of all Israel." And in Exodus 33:11; "The Lord used to speak to Moses face to face, just as a man speaks to his friend." And again in Numbers 12:6-8; "He said, 'Hear now My words: if there is a prophet among you, I, the Lord, shall make Myself known to him in a vision. I shall speak with him in a dream. Not so, with My servant Moses, He is faithful in all My household; with him I speak mouth to mouth, even openly, and not in dark sayings, and he beholds the form of the Lord.'"

The Bible says that when Moses came off of Mt. Sinai, he had to put a veil over his face. There's definite glory in the Old Covenant. We in the New Covenant, though, have it better. "But we all, with unveiled face, beholding as in a mirror the glory of the Lord, are being transformed into the same image from glory to glory, just as from the Lord, the Spirit."

Still, there is a glory that sometimes, even in these revivals, these outpourings of the Spirit that are happening in America and around the world, you go there and they're super-legalistic. Yet, God is moving. There's a glory in the Old Covenant but it's a fading glory. Maybe that's why a lot of these moves of God come and go. In the New Covenant, however, we go from glory to ever-increasing glory.

If Moses can see the face of God in the Old Covenant, how much more can you and I behold it in the New? A pastor said this to me and I've said it ever since. He said, "Ivan, in the Old Covenant if you saw God's face, you would die. But in the New Covenant, if you don't see his face, you'll die." What's interesting about the word "face" is that in the Hebrew, the word *panim* or *paneh* can mean both *face* and *presence*. In Exodus 16:9 when God says to the Israelites, "Come near before the Lord," the word *panim* is used because God is interested in intimacy.

Above all things, the heart of the prophet isn't just to give people prophetic words. It is out of friendship with God that you will encounter his presence and that others around you will encounter his presence. That is the heart of the prophetic ministry!

Abraham was a friend of God. So was Moses, but he also moved in signs and wonders. It's the second type of prophet, if you will, the second part of God's progressive revelation of the prophetic. What I want to emphasize about the Moses type of prophet because Scripture calls him a prophet, is something you also see in Samuel. 1 Samuel 10:25 says, "Then Samuel told the people the ordinances of the kingdom, and wrote them in the book and placed it before the Lord. And Samuel sent all the people away, each one to his house." Where did Samuel find the information to write a book about the behavior of royalty before there were kings? He got it directly from the Lord. In the same way, Moses was taken high up on a mountain and saw the Tabernacle in the realm of the spirit so he would know exactly how to build it. Abraham was close to God but Moses was called to a new level.

Governmental Prophet

Another type of prophet is the governmental or building prophet. Sound similar to the New Covenant apostle? The apostle is the *architekton*, Greek for "master builder," prophets are also listed as part of the foundation of the church in Ephesians 2:20: "Having been built on the foundation of the apostles and prophets, Christ Jesus Himself being the cornerstone."

Apostles and prophets get along really well. Why? Oftentimes, the Lord gives the prophet a blueprint but not an understanding of how to build it. That's where the apostle steps in. I remember speaking to a pastor about his church, sharing what I heard God saying about new phases and what God was going to do. The pastor looked at me and said, "I have everything you just said written out in my office." It was a confirmation that he was building according to the pattern of the Lord.

The prophet carries the spirit of revelation while the apostle carries the spirit of wisdom. It's one of the reasons prophetic people don't do well in religious churches; they don't do well in churches that lack vision. A prophet wants to be part of something with great impact. They want to change the world!

The apostle is like a bull; his head is down to the ground, he's plowing, pioneering, bringing breakthrough in the region. The prophet is like an eagle with eyes to see from above, offering direction to the bull.

This type of prophet can be stubborn, maybe even appear rebellious. This is because most local church's ceilings are merely to have their roles filled: senior pastor, associate pastor, youth pastor, children's pastor, worship pastor, etc. Again, lack of vision. But an apostolic ministry's ceiling is the Kingdom of Heaven itself. The prophet won't struggle with rebellion because she won't feel hemmed in.

Demonstration Prophet

The next type of prophet can be mistaken for an evangelist. This is the Demonstration Prophet, like Elijah and Elisha. They move in signs and wonders. If you see this prophet function and think to yourself, "he moves in healing, he moves in the miraculous… he must be an evangelist," remember that the gift doesn't necessarily identify the calling.

I've ministered several times with Jeff Jansen and we've had a lot of fun. Early on in my ministry, I went to a meeting in Topeka, Kansas in which Jeff prophesied that God told him there would be 90 miles an hour winds that night, something the weather hadn't predicted anything close to, in order to confirm the word of the Lord for the region. The very next day, the newspapers reported on the 90 mph winds that swept through town. That's a Demonstration Prophet. Something in the natural pointed to what God was doing in the spirit.

My friend Chad Dedman tells a story about Bobby Conner. Bobby was ministering and said something like, "Yep, I just believe God wants to demonstrate his power. He just wants to show off!" He pointed to a light and it exploded, Boom! Then he pointed again and Boom! Boom! Boom! Three more lights burst as he pointed to them. Bobby then confessed that the Lord told him, "Boy, you better cut that out! You're going to be in the dark!" Can you imagine having to preach the next session? This type of prophet exists within the Body of Christ today because demonstrations are still needed. Without them, our faith rests on human wisdom and great preaching.

Evangelist Prophet

There is a similar prophet to the Demonstration prophet who, while not necessarily operating in high-level signs and wonders, is equally evangelistic in nature. Patricia King is one of these Evangelist Prophets whose hearts God has wired for the harvest. They constantly prophesy about the harvest to come.

Seer Prophet

Yet another type of prophet is a Seer Prophet like Samuel and Habakkuk. 1 Samuel 9:9 says, "Formerly in Israel, when a man went to inquire of God, he used to say, 'Come, and let us go to the seer;' for he who is called a prophet now was formerly called a seer."

There are several Hebrew words translated to prophet: *nabi* and *nebiah*, or *prophet* and *prophetess* respectively, and *chozeh* and *roeh*, both of which mean *seer*. In the New Testament, they're all one word: prophet. This leads us to think every prophet operates the same. 1 Chronicles 29:29 says, "Now the acts of King David, from first to last, are written in the chronicles of Samuel the seer, in the chronicles of Nathan the prophet and in the chronicles of Gad the seer." Samuel and Gad are both called seers, but separately. That's because, in the Hebrew, they are described by two different words: *chozeh* and *raah*. *Chozeh* means to observe, examine, or to notice, while *raah* is more the classic seer of visions. It's further evidence that not all prophets, even similarly gifted ones, work the same way.

A good example of a Seer Prophet would be Bob Jones who has since passed away. I taught at a prophetic school a few years ago at which Bob Jones also spoke. As I walked forward to do the afternoon session, something hit me in my eye. I said to the young man who was with me, "Listen, I've got to go wash my eye out." I looked in the mirror but there was nothing. I preached my session and afterward took my seat which happened to be in front of Bob. Moments later, I felt a tap on my shoulder. "Boy, I believe I have a warning for you from the Lord!"

I thought, Dear God! I'm not turning around! This is the guy that prophesied they would see God's Eye in the Hubble Telescope. All these major movements; Bethel church, Bethel School of Supernatural Ministry, IHOP… Bob prophesied before they happened I do not want a warning from this guy! "Young man, I saw matter hit you in the eye."

I said, "Sir! That just happened to me before I spoke! Bob, what's the matter?"

He said, "Yep. Exactly, boy. What is the matter? Fear, worry, anxiety, that's what's wrong. You've got eyes just like me. You're called to see. But fear, worry, and anxiety have affected your ability to see."

"What should I do?"

He said, "Imma gonna break it off you, boy." He prayed for me and said, "Here comes the wind!" In the natural, not in the spirit, in the natural, I felt wind and I thought, what the heck is going on? Then he said, "Here comes the anointing!" And I felt like a bucket of something was poured on my chest and I just slid down the chair like a drooling rag doll. Bob said, "An angel was assigned to you today and he will be with you for the rest of your life."

In my mind I asked, "God, can he see it?"

Bob answered out loud, "No, boy, I just sense it."

This kind of prophet is alive and well today. However, we don't hear many stories because we think prophets just speak in conferences. We don't hear the stories of the prophets ministering to presidents and kings because they can't tell you! They can't put that in their newsletters or Facebook, but there are prophets who move in this realm today. Maybe you're called to operate in this realm.

The Seer sees a vision, not only with their eyes closed but often with their eyes open. Consequently, the Seer Prophet is often connected to worship. Elisha, in 2

Kings 3:15, asked for a minstrel before he would prophesy. There's something about worship and the glory of God that permits the Seer to go into a whole different realm. In that realm, they aren't always given an interpretation to their visions, at least not right away. It can be a long wait for the word but a worship atmosphere can help the process along.

The seer may also be a dreamer. Dream interpretations can also be elusive. The most important thing to remember is Genesis 40:8, "Do not interpretations belong to God?" Don't give it your best shot while waiting on God to give it to you. Write down your dreams. Personally, I don't worry about every little detail but God might speak to you in the details. I focus on what sticks out to me and the interpretation usually revolves around that. The second important thing is to keep the word of God deep down on the inside of your heart. It makes sense that God would speak through his word and the more familiar you are with his word, the more open the lines of communication.

Writing Prophet

Another type of prophet is a Writing Prophet. Habakkuk 2:2 says, "Record the vision and inscribe it on tablets, that the one who reads it may run." Rick Joyner may be considered a Writing Prophet. If you've ever heard Rick speak, he's not the most dynamic orator. Read his books, though, like the Final Quest, and they will rock you. Those books came out of encounters he had with the Lord.

Teaching Prophet

Next, we have the Teaching Prophet. Such a prophet is an equipper at heart. A teaching prophet has the ability to break lessons down into practical application and feed it like bread to people. I think a really good Teaching Prophet would be James Goll. Do you ever hear someone try to teach and hear a lot of concept and ideas thrown at you, but by the end, you're left struggling to make sense of it all? A teaching prophet can take something supernatural and revelatory and explain it in such a way that you not only understand but are then able to live it in your own life.

Interceding Prophet

The Interceding Prophet is sometimes called the Watchman. The Hebrew word *shamar* means to *guard* or *keep*. It's the same word the Old Testament uses when the people are told to "keep" the commandments or to "keep" covenant with God. It's also used in Psalms when the psalmist asked God to "keep" him safe. Every local church, family, and ministry should have people they identify as watchmen. These prophetic types tend to operate in the seer dimension of the gift but are nonetheless different than seer prophets.

Not every watchman sees in the spirit but it seems to me to be a common trait among them. These watchmen, also known as prophetic intercessors, are able to see the assignment of the enemy coming against the congregation or the family before it happens. It can be an uncomfortable position to hold, though. Not everyone wants the plans of the enemy laid bare.

When I was in my twenties, I was asked by a church to be a prophet to them. Big responsibility! I've learned that we love the prophetic when it's telling us how good we're doing. But then all of the sudden you can be placed in a leadership position where you say, "Hey listen, last night in a dream the Lord said that you're making this decision because of money and numbers." The Prophet is about righteousness. Who cares about numbers? You can have a lot of people coming to your church, you can have a lot of money, and still not be walking in the divine will of God.

After a while at this church, my voice began to be tuned out more and more. One time I was invited to this business, and it was a multi-million dollar thing. They recognized the prophetic anointing on my life and asked, "Hey, would you do us a favor? We know you hear God. Would you ask the Lord for a word for us?"

I said, "Okay, yeah!" I locked myself away, fasted, and prayed. All of the sudden I saw a vision of a garden hose and water flowing beautifully out of the hose. Then, it was punctured in the side and water began to leak, weakening the flow out of the end. I asked the Lord for an interpretation and he said it was "corruption." I went back to the businessmen and said, "God did speak to me. He said there has been greed among the higher-ups. There has been some corruption and money is actually being pushed out the side and not flowing in the right way."

Turns out the group I spoke to were the higher-ups. Shortly after, the whole thing got shut down by the FBI. Isn't that something? You know, the Lord may put a prophet in your midst, but you've got to listen to him!

Isaiah 62:6 says, "On your walls, O Jerusalem, I have appointed watchmen; all day and all night they will never keep silent..." Watchmen stand guard from high vantage points. If they see the enemy approach, they're responsible for sounding the alarm. "The enemy is coming! The enemy is coming!" Once a watchman has warned the city, his responsibility is over. This is where immature or insecure watchmen get thrown for a loop. If the leaders of the city, the king, or say the apostle, pastor, businessman, whoever it is they are supposed to warn don't heed the warning, the watchman might feel devalued. Or, they might step outside of their role and into that of a soldier, something they aren't built for. What they don't know or understand is that the king has scouts all over the place. The watchmen aren't the only ones on the lookout! The king or leadership may have plans for the enemy that don't involve the watchmen. It's not that their work isn't valued; far from it! But not everyone in a king's service has to know all the king's plans. Jesus even told his followers that, when giving to the poor, "Do not let your left hand know what your right hand is doing," Matthew 6:3. Every part of the body doesn't need to know what every other part is up to in order for it to function properly. So, if you're a watchman, declare what you see then leave the rest to Jesus. Don't attach your identity to the message, or how the message is received, otherwise, you'll walk away dejected. Keep protecting, keep binding, keep loosening, keep interceding, and know that your role is crucial.

Preaching Prophet

Next, we have the Preaching Prophet. These are speakers who you'll hear say, "This isn't the message I prepared for today." I preached at a church once and read somebody's mail entirely by accident. I prayed before hand and asked God for a prophetic word for the church but didn't hear anything. I took the stage, gave my message, and only deviated from my notes as I felt God lead. Afterward, a furious-looking man came up and said, "You gave an example of a guy named this, and that's my name, and you gave an example of this happening and that happening and I couldn't believe that you would expose me and all that had happened in my life until I realized that you don't even know me! The Lord was bringing correction to me through your message and I've got to humble myself."

"I didn't know! Look, here's my notes. I just kind of felt like this was what God was giving me." As the Preaching Prophet speaks, the voice of the Lord flows through him. There are no dreams, no visions, no forewarning, just a revelatory flow as he preaches.

Naba Prophet

Moving on, another kind of prophet is the Naba Prophet. *Naba* means to "bubble forth." The Naba Prophet was pioneered in modern times by Bishop Bill Hamon. If this is you, revelation just sort of spills out of you like a fountain. You can't even help it! Or other times, when you're feeling dry, you're able to "rev" the spirit into motion. "Shanda ba la keleh sek-he," and then you just blow like old faithful and gush revelation all over the place. Sometimes it kick-starts when you place your hand on the person who asked for prayer. Once it gets going, a naba will see picture after picture, word after word. It's how God speaks through them.

God speaks in many different ways. I like to say that God's first language isn't English. It isn't Spanish, or German, or Cantonese, or Tamil. It's the language of the spirit. Find your language with the Holy Spirit and get fluent by speaking with him every day. Sometimes prophetic people sound weird! It's hard being a prophetic person. You wake up in the middle of the night, look at your clock, and it is 1:11. You buy some gum at the store and pay $1.11. All day long, you see 1-1-1 everywhere. I remember this time I preached at an all-black church in New Jersey. An amazing kind of place where you get up, open your bible, and immediately they stand out of honor for the word of God. What I didn't know was I was supposed to say, "You may be seated." As I preached, they continued to stand. I didn't know what was going on! Soon, though, individuals starting hootin' and hollerin' and shouting "Amen!" "Preach it, preacher!" "Glory!" Then the dancing started. And oh man, I was preaching! I mean they pulled the preach out of me! The service was televised so they had these incredibly bright and hot lights. I mean I was burning up from the heat. My mom was there, my wife was there, and after I preached they came over and said, "Your ear is red hot! It's red! Are you okay?"

I said, "I'm just hot because of the lights."

Just then a woman came over to me and said, "I wasn't sure about you at first. I've never heard some of this stuff you were saying. But then the Lord whispered and said, 'Look at his ear.' That's when I knew God was speaking directly to you."

Some months later I was in a conference with James Goll. He and his wife came over and began to pray for me, very dramatically. "Now young man look at me!" Then he smacked me hard in the face! I thought, *you don't smack someone in the face!* I said, "Bro! I got it! You want me to listen! I got it!"

He said, "You're gonna be in meetings and your right ear is going to get red hot with the fire of God."

Excuse me?

"When that happens, it's the gift of faith. Release the miraculous!" God has funny ways of talking to us, but no matter how strange, we've got to get on the same page with him.

Another Hebrew word found in the Old Testament is *nataph*, which means "to cause to drop, one drop at a time like individual drops of rain." Judges 5:4 uses this word when it says, "Lord, when You went out from Seir, when You marched from the field of Edom, the earth quaked, the heavens also dripped, even the clouds dripped water." It is also used as a manner of speaking, to "drop" a word from the Lord on someone, like in Ezekiel 20:46.

Some prophets drop revelation like this, slow and steady. In comparison, the Naba Prophet is like a chihuahua hooked up on caffeine. They're prophesying fast! This *nataph*-style prophet you often see manifest in worship. Psalm 22:3 says God is "enthroned upon the praises of Israel." God inhabits the praises of his people. Another great Hebrew word is *tehillah* which means spontaneous praise. Have you ever sung a song so many times that you can sing it without thinking? There comes a point where you detach from the lyrics and you're sort of on autopilot while your mind wanders. Something happens, a lot of musicians are sensitive to it, where that *nataph*, the rain of the Holy Spirit—not a downpour but drops—falls and revelation falls with it. I love to have prophets on the worship team when this happens. They begin to sing and it's one phrase after another. "The Lord's releasing joy in this place right now! He's imparting hope to you! Hope deferred makes the heart sick but desire come to pass is like a tree of life! Lord, we thank you for hope! I see you planted like a tree of life! Planted by the rivers of water! You produce fruit in every season. No longer tossed to and fro! No longer, but rooted and grounded in the love of God!"

It's the same thing with the teaching anointing. I could be in the middle of teaching, writing on a white board, everyone taking notes when all of the sudden the Spirit of the Lord shifts and I begin to prophesy. "My children, my children! It is time to rise up and be bold and courageous! God is awakening a generation, shaking off the chains of apathy, breaking off the spirit of religion, overcoming poverty! Rise up, sons and daughters of God! It's time to let your light shine before men!" It went to another level. It passed from the realm of intellect into the spirit realm. And there is this *nataph*, this prophetic anointing, which doesn't only flow through praise and worship but it's a good place to start. Haven't you ever been waiting on the Holy Spirit, soaking and asking the Father to speak to you, when suddenly you got a thought: Boop! Like a drop of rain! And like a drop of rain, it's refreshing!

Massah Prophet

Another type of prophet, or at least a way some prophets receive revelation, is *massah*. *Massah* means, "what is lifted, a burden, a message." These prophets feel a burden from the Lord and they may not know exactly what it is until they pray it through. It is important for these types of prophets to pray through the burden before releasing it in order to gain understanding. It isn't a bad burden, like a secret sin, but a piece of God's heart, heavy for his people. These prophets are those who prostrate themselves before God and press in. "Father! In Jesus' name, I feel this burden. God, what's grieving your heart right now? I want to understand." God eventually reveals his heart which releases the prophet to release the word, lifting the burden.

Early in my ministry, it doesn't happen as much anymore, before the Lord spoke to me I would weep. I'd just be sitting in a service and out of nowhere start to cry. Then, I'd get revelation. I wondered, "Is this what happened to Jeremiah?" We call him the weeping prophet because of what was happening in the land, but I wonder... We've been so afraid of emotion! "Don't be emotional," we're told. I say, if you cut off your emotions, you will cut off the flow of the Spirit of God in your life. God is not afraid of your emotions. Jesus may well weep along with you while you weep for others. There are times when you pray for someone, you'll feel what they're feeling. Don't be afraid of emotions. It's just another way God speaks to his prophets.

Hopefully, you've identified yourself in one of these prophetic types. Maybe you thought you were the only one who felt the way you did. Maybe you thought you were weird or unusual. You are not alone. Prophets of all shapes, sizes, and styles have existed for thousands of years. And you may be weird, but so am I! That's how God made you.

CHAPTER FOUR

"Prophets: True or False"

There are certain levels of the prophetic that are easy to get comfortable with. It's easy just talking about edification, exhortation, and comfort, giving simple words of encouragement to one another. Then you have these really weird, strange people who claim they hear Jesus' audible voice and have encounters with him. They have basic impressions but they also see visions, dream dreams, go into trances, and even have angelic visitations. When we reach that level of prophetic ministry, people unfamiliar with the prophetic or religious people don't know what to make of it. Really, they're afraid. They're afraid of deception, of being deceived by the enemy. To be honest, there are some good reasons to be afraid. Cults have formed around angelic appearances. Paul warned the Colossians against the worship, or "religion" of angels in chapter two verse 18. We'll come back around to that a little later.

Angelic Visitations

In 2005 I had an angelic encounter. I was asleep in my room when the Lord woke me up. Understand, I am not a light sleeper. I can't even soak in the spirit. As soon as lie down on my back, I'm snoring. But this night, it was like God injected caffeine into my veins and I was immediately wide awake. I got really worked up because I knew God was about to speak to me. I had to be quiet, though, because my wife and little baby were still sleeping. I felt the Holy Spirit whisper to me, "Go outside," so I went out onto the balcony. I took a few deep breaths to relax myself when all of the sudden I saw someone sitting in a tree outside my home. Their features were neither male nor female, though it looked to me like a boy whose hair was in tight curls. This angel held a silver trumpet which it brought to its lips and sounded. I heard an alarm go off like an ambulance was driving by. The angel smiled at me, then disappeared.

"Wait!" I hear some of you saying. "If you really saw an angel, you know what it says in Daniel, you'd fall like a dead man!" Valid point. It does happen in scripture that when some men see angels, they fall like dead men. Women, on the other hand, tend to respond differently. They see an angel and ask questions. Maybe it depends on the level of glory in which the angel chooses to manifest, or maybe the Lord chooses. In my encounter, there was no fear. "Well, was it in the spirit or in the natural?" It can be hard to distinguish between the two. Did I see the angel with my open eyes? Yes. Did it look like flesh and blood? It looked like nothing from this world!

The encounter took longer for you to read about than it did to happen. My unrenewed mind said, "You did not just see an angel sitting in a tree with a silver trumpet. You've lost it! Go back to sleep!" I ignored that thought and instead asked God, "Are you speaking to me?"

I heard, "Numbers 10:9."

Memorizing scripture is a good practice to get into. I've got a lot of scripture memorized but I admit not much of it is from Numbers. I opened my Bible and read, and sure enough, the verse was about the trumpet! Numbers 10:9 says, "When you go to war in your land against the adversary who attacks you, then you shall sound an alarm with the trumpets, that you may be remembered before the Lord your God, and be saved from your enemies." The trumpet was used to mobilize people; it's how you get their attention. During that time, I had a youth ministry that was quickly growing A word was brewing in me about it being time to advance and I knew God was calling a generation to greater things. The visitation confirmed the word.

Not long after, I had another encounter. I was still a youth director and the youth were leading the service that day. I sat in the back watching them like a proud papa. Suddenly an angel appeared right in front of me. With one wing it covered its face and a hand came out holding a burning-hot ember. It was so hot that I could feel it and I jumped back! Once again, it disappeared. It happened faster than I'd be able to tell you about it, and I speak quickly! I turned to the person sitting next to me and said, "I just saw an angel."

The guy scooted his chair away from me.

I fell on my face. I didn't have any understanding. The Lord didn't speak anything to me. It scared me because this time it wasn't a gentle young man sitting in a tree; this was intense! Eventually, I realized God was speaking to me out of Isaiah 6. "In the year of King Uzziah's death I saw the Lord sitting on a throne, lofty and exalted, with the train of His robe filling the temple. Seraphim stood above Him, each having six wings: with two he covered his face, and with two he covered his feet, and with two he flew. And one called out to another and said,

'Holy, Holy, Holy, is the Lord of hosts, the whole earth is full of His glory."...
Then I said,

'Woe is me, for I am ruined! Because I am a man of unclean lips, and I live among a people of unclean lips; for my eyes have seen the King, the Lord of hosts.' Then one of the Seraphim flew to me with a burning coal in his hand, which he had taken from the altar with tongs. He touched my mouth with it and said, 'Behold, this has touched your lips; and your iniquity is taken away and your sin is forgiven.'"

I felt like the Lord asked me a question; "Will you embrace the fire?" In some services, in some Christian groups, we shout "Fire! Fire of God," when the Spirit really heats up. *Will I embrace the fire?* Listen, that coal was HOT! I realized that this wasn't a fire that was going to play around. This was that Malachi 3:2 refiner's fire the purified the sons and daughters of Levi. I hesitated to answer God. Finally, I said, "All right, Lord. I say 'Yes' to the fire."

I then entered one of the hardest seasons of my entire life. During that time I had a dream in which I was at the home of a minister named Rodney Howard Browne. He played a CD for me that filled his house with the glory of God. In the dream, I lied down and change fell from my pocket. Then the spirit that rested on Rodney rested on me and I began to laugh. I'm good friends with one of Rodney's sons so, after I woke from the dream, I called and asked him what he thought it meant. He said, "That's partly for you and partly for Rodney. He's releasing a CD and is nervous because he is singing on it."

He called Rodney who then invited me to the Winter Camp Meeting. Another pastor named Denny Cline and I attended. Rodney didn't know what I looked like but during the first session he called me out from the crowd. "Young man, stand out in the aisle... Fire!" I got hit with the fire of God. The next session: ""Young man, stand out in the aisle... Fire!" Wham! I got hit again. This happened six or seven times until Denny finally asked, "What is going on with you, Rodney, and the fire of God?" After that meeting, Denny invited Rodney to his church and thousands of people were saved in the region, all because of that dream. On one level, the fire of God was doing some impressive stuff, but it working on my heart at the same time. God was dealing with things I thought I'd confessed and dealt with long ago. The fire purged so much impurity from my heart. It was a challenging season.

Right after that season ended, I was invited to speak at a youth conference, the title of which was Isaiah Six! I thought, *I'm being set up for something!* Not to mention it was a United Methodist conference. When I got up to speak, the fire of God hit those young people. I ministered without any hype, without any shouting, just "Holy Spirit, come." Kids fell out on the floor, wept, and cried out in repentance. The fire of God had to purge me before it could flow through my ministry.

Fast-forward a few years and I was watching some teaching videos at home. Except it's never just one thing with me. I'm really A.D.D. so it was probably the teaching video, Facebook, music, and Netflix going. My wife doesn't understand how I manage to get any work done but somehow I do. I was listening to Louise Lopez teach when she had her listeners do this activation of inviting angels into the room. Let me clarify, even though I'd had angelic visitations, I'd never asked for them. So I was listening to Louise lead this activation, and I was half-heartedly participating while doing five other things. I said, "Lord, show me the angels in the room." Immediately I'm onto something different, messaging somebody on Facebook. All of the sudden, at the foot of my bed, in the realm of the spirit, I see an angel. This time it was not holding a silver trumpet at its side but was pressing the trumpet to its lips while standing at attention. I thought, *Oh I better focus up, here.* I knew something was about to happen.

Louise went on to say, "Ask the angel its name." If the angel or God gives you the angel's name, study what the name means. Often the name's meaning is what the Father is doing.

Names were important in Hebrew culture. You didn't name your son one of the top-ten fad names going around. What you'd do is the Lord would speak to you and you'd name babies based on the word of the Lord. Basically, you prophesied destiny over your children based on the name. I had never asked the Lord to give me the name of an angel but in this latest encounter I heard the name, "Benoni."

I thought, *Man, all those years of marijuana and drug use before I was saved, I'm having some type of weird flashback here! Benoni?* Then I realized I could no longer hear Louise. The Father's presence filled the room and I began to weep. That is often a manifestation when I feel the presence of God. The Lord spoke to me and said, "No longer do I call you Benoni; I call you Benjamin. No longer do I call you 'son of my suffering.' You've said that everything you've ever had, you had to fight for. I say today that I call you Benjamin, the son of my right hand, the son of my inheritance!" The Lord began to deal with me about this fighter mentality I had. He then spoke out loud, "Jacob! Why are you still wrestling?"

I thought, *Well, that's what revival preachers preach!* "You've got to be like Jacob and you've got to wrestle with God! You wrestle with God throughout the day, and you wrestle with God until you have a limp, and you wrestle with God until he blesses you." And boy, I've preached that myself. I'm from the east coast, I can get everybody standing, stomping their heels, and sweating. But God's question to me was "Why are you still wrestling?" I thought, *That's all I know. All I've ever known is how to fight!* The Lord spoke to me again and said, "Will you let me give you your inheritance?" Ephesians 1:11 sprang to mind. He then said, "You have obtained."

65

Shortly after this experience, I can't say who because they wish to remain anonymous, but someone came to me and said, "We would like to bless you with an early inheritance. We would like to bless you to be able to get your own home." What they probably didn't know was that only weeks prior I sat at a coffee shop crying out to God. "It is so hard here! You've called me to plant a church and I've sacrificed everything. We've given up our savings account, Lord, and we've done everything to come and establish this ministry and the work here and nothing is breaking through! Did I hear right? Is this really my home?"

Just then, a song came on my Pandora radio station by the secular artist Phillip Phillips. "Hold on to me as we go as we roll down this unfamiliar road. And although this wave is stringing us along, just know you're not alone, cause I'm going to make this place your home." I nearly lost it right there in the middle of a coffee shop. At the time, our income wasn't very much. The houses we could afford, I wasn't comfortable leaving behind my wife and kids in those neighborhoods when I traveled. My wife, who has more faith than me, was looking at house $10,000 and even $20,000 outside our price range. I was feeling less and less like a man, unable to provide for my family! We found a house we liked, that my kids instantly felt at home in, and of course, it was way too expensive. I was getting sick to my stomach and I think the real estate agent noticed. She was a believer who attended our church. She said to me, "Remember, pastor; faith!"

Oh, yeah. Faith, right? So we put in an offer. A very low offer. And it was accepted. Trouble was, I couldn't afford the monthly payments! I felt terrible. *What am I doing to my family? I've got them in poverty!* I went for a walk and the Lord spoke to me: "Son, do you want that home?"

"Yes, Lord!"

"Then ask me for it."

I was whining and complaining, and the Jacob in me was ready to go and get another job or start another business. The problem with my personality type is, if I don't feel God moving, I'm going to do the moving for him. All the while though, he's asking, "Will you let me be your father and provide for you?" I told my wife we were supposed to ask God for the home. We held hands and did just that.

The next day, we got a call from our real estate agent. "I'm here getting my nails done and I just got a phone call from the mortgage broker. My hairs are standing up! Chills! The selling agent, who's selling the house for his parents, he's a believer, and he said he wants to help you get into the house. He refused a commission and wants to give a sizable portion of the house's cost back at closing. Then the broker, he decided to lower his fee to help the seller. The insurance agent heard what was going on and decided to lower his rate, too. And you know what? I've decided I don't really need a full commission, either."

I asked, "How many years have you been doing real estate?"

"Forty years."

"In all that time, have you ever heard about anything like this happening?"

"Never in my life." God promised he'd give me a home. It's the home I'm living in now. I'm living in a home I couldn't afford. But he could, and now so can I because he gave me an inheritance! All kick-started by an angelic visitation. God used angels to bring messages in the Bible and he's still doing it today. I believe many of you have had messages from God brought by angels only maybe you just didn't see them.

False Prophets vs. Young or Immature Prophets

Whenever someone talks about angelic visitations at a conference or meeting, right away I feel something in the spirit realm. I feel listeners shut off their hearts, put up all their walls of defense, and say to themselves, "Uh-oh. Heresy." No, it's New Covenant Christianity! If it wasn't for the angelic, what would have happened to baby Jesus? There are angels throughout the Bible from Genesis to Revelation. Our minds need to be renewed with Kingdom revelation so that we can see the angelic for what it is. An unrenewed mind can't accept radical and supernatural events as Godly.

The Lord wants us to expect him to speak to us. What would happen if when we go to church or even Starbucks, that we realize we are carriers of an open heaven and that Christ lives in us? How different would we be? How ready to listen and act? Instead, we ask ourselves, "Where are you in the room right now, Jesus? What are you doing, God?" It's a different mindset when we expect God to interact with us on a regular and personal basis.

Still, 1 John 4:1-3 says, "Beloved, do not believe every spirit, but test the spirits to see whether they are from God because many false prophets have gone out into the world. By this you know the Spirit of God: every spirit that confesses that Jesus Christ has come in the flesh is from God; and every spirit that does not confess Jesus is not from God; this is the spirit of the antichrist, of which you have heard that it is coming, and now it is already in the world."

Expect God to speak to you but don't expect every supernatural encounter or voice you hear to be from the Lord. Tests the spirits. Don't be afraid to ask questions.

Then in Deuteronomy 18:20-22, "But the prophet who speaks a word presumptuously in My name which I have not commanded him to speak, or which he speaks in the name of other gods, that prophet shall die.' You may say in your heart, 'How will we know the word which the Lord has not spoken?' When a prophet speaks in the name of the Lord, if the thing does not come about or come true, that is the thing which the Lord has not spoken. The prophet has spoken it presumptuously; you shall not be afraid of him."

That's some pretty strong language. If a prophet's word doesn't come to pass, he should die? If a prophet's word doesn't come true, he's a false prophet? "Ivan, didn't you just write in chapter two that New Covenant Prophets are allowed to miss it and live? Didn't you say none of us have mastered hearing God and none of us get it right 100% of the time? Which is it?"

First, let's remember this advice was under the Old Covenant and God's people were governed by laws, not grace. Under the New Covenant, we interpret these instructions as one way to test a word from the Lord. If a prophet's words consistently fail to come to pass or produce fruit, maybe those words weren't from God. A single missed word doesn't make a false prophet. When you're given a word by a prophet, test it. Is it in-line with the nature and character of God? If so, receive it. Did it ever come to pass? If so, chances are that prophet is the real deal.

Young prophets can miss it because they're still practicing. It's okay. Don't be alarmed. It's one reason testing the word is so important. It's also why the church has come up with so many guidelines for the prophetic. If you've spent any time on a church prayer team you might already be familiar: no dates, no mates, no babies, no direction, and no correction. Now, I'll admit, I do some of those sometimes. I offer correction. It's not necessarily wrong to prophesy any of these things. But before you do, ask yourself, are you in the right position? Whose position is it to offer correction? Usually, it's a father or mother. God corrects his children as we've already discussed. Are you a father or mother figure to whomever you're correcting? If not, it might not be appropriate. I invite fathers and mothers to speak into my life, as should you. But I don't allow just anybody to speak into me. Even if you see something clear as a bell over someone, let your relationship and the Holy Spirit guide what you release.

Untested prophetic words are risky. Bob Jones once told me, "Boy, you need to stop letting them prophets live your life!" I thought, *You're the prophet of prophets and you're telling me to stop listening to prophets?* Another prophet friend of mine called and said, "Ivan, I had a vision of you going through your filing cabinet and you were talking out all of these prophetic words you'd received. You were asking the Lord, 'Does this word pass? Is this for a future time? Or was this word never from you? Was it just flattery?'" She went on to say, "I saw God speaking to you and saying, 'That word has been fulfilled but it didn't look the way you thought it was going to look.' And, 'this is a future word.' And, 'this is for the season that you're in now.' And, 'some of these words you just need to throw away because they were never from me.'"

People are fearful. We say, "Put it on the shelf," but some words need to be flushed down the toilet! God will rarely give you revelation from a source with which you have no relationship. Testing is one thing but he doesn't want you second-guessing. True revelation will come from a place of safety and trust.

Prophets: True or False

I was in a church service one time and I was gonna get up there and bring revival by myself. That whole year I fasted every other day. I was pacing back and forth, really pressing in and going for it when I felt a tug on my shirt. I looked down and this cute little boy said, "Why can't you just be a kid?" That hit me like an arrow in my heart. Why can't I just be like a kid? True, I didn't know the child but the source was still a place of safety and trust. It was a kid for crying out loud!

If you feel a check or a caution when being given a word, it's okay for you to put up a boundary and say, "I'm sorry, could you write that word down," or even, "I just don't feel comfortable receiving this."

Early on in my ministry, I was at Mt. Shasta doing outreach when a strange dude with a shovel over his shoulder walked toward me. He said, "I see colors over you." He prophesied using colors. "I see the color purple over you and the color blue over you. Purple represents the calling that you have with your God. And blue represents the gifts that you operate in." At the time, I was really confused about my calling and there I was, being prophesied over by a new-ager! It didn't help my confusion because there was a measure of truth in what he said. Blue often represents the prophetic and purple represents sonship and the apostolic. It messed me up so much that I had to get inner-healing prayer! Be careful who you let speak into your life.

That is not being rude; that's establishing boundaries.

One of the first prophetic words I received was from a well-known prophet who sat me down and asked, "What's the Lord speaking to you young man?"

I proceeded to go on and on about what God was speaking to me about Enoch, how his name meant "consecration and dedication," how he was a prophet, about how the life he lived was an example to other prophets, and more revelation I'd received about the manifest sons of God. After I'd finished, the prophet said, "Wow, young man! You know, you hear the Lord very clearly."

"Thank you," I said. But in my heart, I was secretly saying *I know.*

"You know you're also very arrogant, don't you?" He asked.

For some of you, that would break your heart. My background, though, is in full-contact fighting. Literally. If you and I are sparring and you never throw a punch at me, you're wasting my time. For me to become a better fighter, I need you to try to hit me in the face so I can learn how to block and dodge. Early on, pastors used to try and correct me by telling me stories, like, "Remember what Nathan said to David about a rich man and a poor man and their sheep? Now the rich man…" I'd leave that meeting and have no idea what they were trying to tell me. I'm a straight shooter. If you want to tell me something, tell me. "Ivan, let me tell you story about a boy who…" does nothing for me. But sit me down and say, "Hey Ivan, you're a little cocky," and I get the message. It's how God speaks to me, too. He speaks to us all in ways that match our personalities.

It can sometimes go along with a prophet's personality that we think we're the only ones who hear from God and can speak for him. Not true. All believers can hear his voice. Those fathers and mothers I was talking about? They don't have to be prophets. They don't have to be five-fold gifted. They just need to know Jesus and know you.

Back to this idea of "no dates, no mates." Say you're practicing and you're getting pretty confident. You see marriage over someone and you're sure that you're sure that you've got it right. There have been so many "prophetic" situations where somebody prophesied a marriage and was so off. But, the person got married because they felt like they had to obey the voice of the Lord and it ended up in destruction. Listen; he who finds a wife finds favor. Just let them do the finding. Still sure God showed you? Fine. Write it down and keep it to yourself.

When I was a student at Bethel School of Supernatural Ministry in 2001-02, a prophet named David Saunders visited and ministered. Four years later, my wife-to-be Erica, we were engaged at the time, ended up house sitting for him. I went with her to see him after all those years, not having spoken to him in that time. I walked in and in his British accent he said, "Ivan! Stay right here!" He ran off, grabbed his journal, opened it and read, "Ivan, the Lord has been having me pray for your wife."

"What name does it say in that book?"

"Erica. What's your fiancé's name?"

"Erica!"

God had him praying for Erica before I ever met an Erica, before I ever met my wife! So yes, God can show you these things, but often it's to confirm a thing after the fact. If I had been told four years earlier I was going to marry an Erica, I may have married the wrong one! Or married the right one too soon!

Don't use the prophetic to meddle in other people's lives. That's manipulation and control. We're under a new covenant where there are no rules. Guidelines, yes. But no rules. Because *he* rules. We want the Holy Spirit to lead people, not a spirit of control.

Discerning a False Prophet

In Acts 16, a woman followed Luke and Paul, declaring, "These men are bond-servants of the Most High God, who are proclaiming to you the way of salvation." She did this for days until Paul finally got so annoyed he cast the devil right out of her. How did Paul discern it was a demon's work since the revelation it shouted was true? Just because a word is true doesn't mean it is coming from the Lord Jesus Christ, born of a virgin, Son of the Living God, who died on a cross, and rose on the third day.

1. Test the Spirits

Accuracy isn't the only test of prophetic purity. Accuracy isn't the only test to discern the source. Paul was in constant communion with the Holy Spirit, that's how he knew. Jesus prayed that we and God would be one. We need to hear directly from the Holy Spirit to rightly discern. If you have a second-heaven encounter and you're not yet able to discern who's visiting you, my advice would be to plead the blood of Jesus. Ask them to confess Jesus as their Lord, or command them to go if they weren't sent in Jesus' name. 1 John 4:1-3 says, "Beloved, do not believe every spirit, but test the spirits to see whether they are from God, because many false prophets have gone out into the world. By this you know the Spirit of God: every spirit that confesses that Jesus Christ has come in the flesh is from God; and every spirit that does not confess Jesus is not from God; this is the spirit of the antichrist, of which you have heard that it is coming, and now it is already in the world."

How many of you women reading this have ever shaken a man's hand and immediately wanted to wash yours afterward? You may have discerned an unclean spirit without realizing. "Who may ascend into the hill of the Lord? Or who may stand in His holy place? He who has clean hands and a pure heart," says Psalms 24:3-4. With the indwelling of the Holy Spirit comes the ability to discern spirits. As with all things, it gets better with practice.

I ministered once in Newfoundland, Canada and stayed at an old bed and breakfast owned by a pastor. I was 20 at the time, still not very old in the Lord. It's embarrassing to admit but I was also afraid of the dark. I used to get tormented in the night by demonic visitations. I was too scared to tell anybody because I was a world champion martial artist. I'd competed and medaled in Korea. I was a tough dude! I don't look it anymore but back then I was ripped! People like me weren't supposed to be scared of the dark. I got up to use the downstairs bathroom and had every light on and the bathroom door open so I could see anything approaching. All of the sudden I see a woman floating down the stairs! Interestingly, though, I didn't feel fear. The peace of the Holy Spirit came upon me and he said, "Rebuke it."

That's what I want you to remember; not that I saw a demon but that the peace of God came on me and gave me authority. When we talk about the supernatural people get so afraid and focus on the demons themselves. No. Focus on the power of God in you to rebuke the enemy. And that's what I did. "I command you to go in the name of Jesus!" At once it disappeared.

The next day I told my mentor the story. He said, "I didn't want to tell you but I was freaking out earlier! I could tell there was demonic stuff in this house." Later at dinner, I spoke to the pastor and asked, "Was there a woman, an elderly woman, looked sort of like this, who died here years ago?"

"Yes! That's the legend, anyway. Why do you ask?"

My mentor said, "There was a familiar spirit here. Ivan saw it and cast it out."

Prophets: True or False

There's a progression from basic prophecy—God loves you and has a plan for your life—to Level Two Prophet, so to speak, where you begin to deal with principalities and powers. God opens your eyes and suddenly you're casting out familiar spirits.

There's a story in one of John G. Lake's books. A mom and dad grieve the loss of a child. I can't even go there in my mind, to know what that feels like. They were so distraught they went to a spirit medium who conjured up the little girl. Convinced they were talking to their little girl, they told pastor John G. Lake of the experience. Lake responded that he'd love to go back to the medium with them and see for himself. Once there, the medium again conjured the "little girl" who spoke in her voice and knew specifics about her. Lake, though, asked if the girl remembered the day at church she gave her life to Jesus. The medium immediately starting screaming "No! No!" Lake commanded the demon out of the medium, shutting down his business. The spirit was accurate, so much so that the parents were convinced it was their daughter. But the source was suspect, and Lake could discern the spirits. We need to be able to do the same.

This kind of thing happens, even today. It's really only the western church, North America and Western Europe, that struggles with believing the supernatural. I've been to Haiti, to the house of a witch doctor; I've been to Africa, Ecuador, Peru, all over the world. When you start talking about the supernatural, they've experienced it. We have our own demonic spirits in the west: spirits of humanism, unbelief, over-intellectualization, and materialism to name a few. But there's power in the name of Jesus. The gospel is power!

2. A Different Gospel

Galatians 1:8-9 says, "But even if we, or an angel from heaven, should preach to you a gospel contrary to what we have preached to you, he is to be accursed! As we have said before, so I say again now, if any man is preaching to you a gospel contrary to what you received, he is to be accursed!" When I was a youth pastor, I knew someone who really wanted an angelic visitation and finally experienced some encounters. However, they were struggling with some things which left doors open to unwelcome guests. The "angels" told this person they didn't have to read the Bible, instead, "We'll tell you everything about Jesus that you need to know." Big red flag right there! If you want to grow in the supernatural and experience the Kingdom of God, you need to go deeper into the word! Those demonic spirits also said, "We don't want you to go to church anymore. We want to spend time with you all alone." Isn't that interesting? "Don't read your bible and isolate yourself from community." I've heard so many Christians say, "I don't need to go to church, I am the church." Not by yourself, you're not. *We* are the church. We are many parts but one body.

There's a spirit of independence trying to break its way into the church. "I am the church. I don't have to gather anymore. I don't need the bible. I have the word of God in me." Deception! The church needs a reality check. If the message is contrary to what's written in the Word, if it is not the gospel of Jesus Christ, I don't care how beautiful the angel was or how amazing the encounter was, you're listening to a demon.

3. Check the Fruit

Matthew 7:15-19 says, "Beware of the false prophets, who come to you in sheep's clothing, but inwardly are ravenous wolves. You will know them by their fruits. Grapes are not gathered from thorn bushes nor figs from thistles, are they? So every good tree bears good fruit, but the bad tree bears bad fruit. A good tree cannot produce bad fruit, nor can a bad tree produce good fruit. Every tree that does not bear good fruit is cut down and thrown into the fire. So then, you will know them by their fruits."

Outside of accuracy, the fruit a prophet produces can also be what he does with the revelation he receives. I remember one time when working in a youth ministry, this man walked up to me and I saw the word "pedophile" written over his head. I felt like I was a horrible person who didn't know how to love. I beat myself up because I believed the prophetic was meant to pull the best out of people and there I was defining the man by his sin. Finally, I met with the pastor and, stammering and mumbling, I confessed to him what I'd seen. He said, "You're right! He had this court thing and he had to have permission to be here. Why do you think God showed you this?"

"I have no clue."

"What are you doing here?"

"Helping out with the youth ministry."

"Exactly! Love him, but don't let him serve with the youth!"

I could have told the man what I'd seen, embarrassing him and crushing his soul. That's bad fruit. Instead, I kept the revelation to myself in order to produce good fruit by loving him while protecting both him and the youth. The Lord will show you discernment and he will warn you but we don't want critical spirits. We need to learn how to love through the revelation we receive.

4. The End Result

Proverbs 14:12 says, "There is a way which seems right to a man, but its end is the way of death." There's an old saying: You're headed where you're going. People are afraid of the prophetic partly because of tragic stories of false prophets. Most people are at least partially familiar with the story of Joseph Smith and his supposed angelic visitation. An "angel" named Moroni visited Joseph and told him about a book written on gold plates that contained the fullness of the gospel. Joseph also claimed he was visited by John the Baptist. Through these and many other encounters, Joseph Smith founded the Church of Jesus Christ of Latter Day Saints or Mormonism. These are the ones who'll visit your house in white shirts and ties. They've actually stopped coming to my house because I'll sit with them and ask questions: "Do you believe you can feel the presence of the Holy Spirit? Do you believe in the gifts of the Holy Spirit?" They do believe in miracles and in Jesus. Yet they have no foundation in the true written word of God which allows room for deception. As I continued to ask more and more questions, they decided to scratch my address off their books. I guess I'm a lost cause! One guy, though, did say he thought I was a prophet. The thing is, they don't believe has the ability to hear God for themselves. They think that only certain are appointed as prophets and apostles to hear the voice of God for the entire movement.

Without a firm grasp on scripture, there's so much room for deception. They believe everyone, humans, angels, even Lucifer and Jesus, are all God's children and we're all equals prior to life on Earth. Satan is not equal to Jesus. No one is equal to Jesus! He is God! The King of Kings and Lord of Lords!

Now, it's entirely possible there are some Mormons who've come to a place and said, "Jesus, I believe you died on the cross and you rose from the dead." Perhaps their theology isn't perfect, but will we see them in heaven? I do believe that! I believe we're going to be surprised by who we see in heaven. However, this is a good example of somebody who was duped by a counterfeit angel and an entire cult was formed around it.

One way to avoid the trap of the "way that seems right to a man" is to have humility. As a senior pastor, I've had more people try to speak into my life than I've ever wished. After a while, it can get overwhelming. But, outside of the boundaries I've already discussed, I love it because it can keep me humble. I'm not the only person God speaks to about my church, or my life for that matter.

If your response to someone telling you, "Your zipper has been down the whole evening" is "No, it's not! It's the new style," you need to learn humility. Ever heard someone say "you don't know what's in my heart?" Sure I do. Jesus discerned what laid within the hearts of men. Luke 6:45 says, "...out of the abundance of the heart his mouth speaks." I can ask you one question, and based on your answer, know exactly what's in your heart.

Humility is important. It doesn't matter how gifted we are, or how accurate; if our character is out of whack, if we're filled with pride, independence, or rebellion, people aren't going to trust the revelation we give them. We need to pause occasionally and ask ourselves, " Am I acting like a know-it-all simply because God told me something?"

I've encountered people who act in the following manner, telling me: "You know I've attended seven different churches in the area!"

"Wow," I'd say. "Why so many churches?"

"I'm a prophet. I go to a church and God shows me all of the sin there and everything the pastor is doing wrong. I tell that pastor and then they reject me! So I shake the dust off of my feet and go to the next church. It's just like the Bible says; a prophet isn't without honor except in their hometown."

I want so badly to sit them down and, with all the love in the world, tell them, "You're not being rejected because you're a prophet. It's because you're acting like a jerk!" The role of the prophet, along with the rest of church leadership, is to *serve the church.* That isn't accomplished by a stranger telling an entire congregation their sin. If you meet someone like this, and they're looking to get involved in your church, ask them to start with some light cleaning after Bible Study or taking out the trash on Thursdays. If the Son of God, in John 13, can get on one knee to wash the feet of his disciples but this self-proclaimed prophet won't lower themselves to taking out the trash, invite them to find humility or find another church.

Character

Tests of character and tests of the heart are critical to pass in order to go deeper. It's got nothing to do with age but for some of us, it takes a little longer to learn. When Moses discovered he was a Hebrew, he tried to respond with the arm of the flesh and he struck a man dead. He said to himself, "I got this. Forget about that not-by-might, not-by-power spirit. I can do this without God." For that, God sent him to the backside of the wilderness for 40 years. Then when God called Moses up, Moses stuttered and said, "I can't even talk right!" He had to be broken and humbled before he could be used by God. Hopefully, it doesn't take you 40 years to learn the lesson! There are those whose hearts are so tender that when they hear the Holy Spirit they say, "Yes, Lord!"

On the road to Damascus, Saul of Tarsus believed he knew the Word better than most. He had the Torah memorized, a student of Gamaliel. All of the sudden the Lord Jesus spoke to Saul in Acts Nine: "As he was traveling, it happened that he was approaching Damascus, and suddenly a light from heaven flashed around him; and he fell to the ground and heard a voice saying to him, "Saul. Saul, why are you persecuting Me?" And he said, "Who are You, Lord?" And He said, "I am Jesus whom you are persecuting, but get up and enter the city, and it will be told you what you must do." The men who traveled with him stood speechless, hearing the voice but seeing no one. Saul got up from the ground, and though his eyes were open, he could see nothing; and leading him by the hand, they brought him into Damascus. And he was three days without sight, and neither ate nor drank. Now there was a disciple at Damascus named Ananias; and the Lord said to him in a vision, 'Ananias.' And he said, 'Here I am, Lord.'"

The Lord came to a certain disciple. Not a big shot. Not a well-known minister with books and a Twitter following. His response to Jesus calling his name? "Here I am, Lord!" Saul, on the other hand, a big shot, demands to know, "Who are you?"

It's crucial if in church leadership to get healed up on the inside. I'm an inner-healing junkie; I love it! We've all got junk on the inside: rebellion, pride, abandonment, whatever. If you're afraid to be vulnerable and transparent, that's when the enemy places his hooks. Jesus said in John 14:30, "...the ruler of the world [Satan] is coming, and he has nothing in Me." There was nothing in the heart of Jesus that the devil could snare. I want a heart like that! I don't want to walk around in unforgiveness, bitterness, or spiritual pride. I want to walk in such humility that the Holy Spirit flows through me and when Papa says, "Ivan, don't do that," or "Ivan, do this," I say, "Yes Lord." And I don't want it to take me 40 years to get there!

Removing Fear

When it comes to the prophetic and the supernatural, I've noticed that the enemy plants seeds of fear in people starting at a young age. Little kids start to see and experience the demonic and it's not the parents' fault. They don't even know. They say, "Oh, you're just imagining these things. You're fine. There are no ghosts in your room!" Maybe there aren't. But maybe a demonic spirit is harassing your child. I'm not someone who sees demons behind every corner but the reality is, they are out there. Knowing this, I started teaching my boys to pray with authority at an early age.

I heard a story from Brian Johnson, Bill Johnson's son. He said that when he was a little boy he was tormented in the night. His dad would come to him and say,

"Okay son. In the midst of your fear I want to teach you how to praise God." They would sing hymns together, this little boy with his broken voice and his dad. They'd sing and sing until they felt the peace of God, and then Brian would go to sleep. Bill trained his child spiritual warfare through worship. I love that! That's what we need to do in our families, too.

A lot of children grow up tormented. Maybe you were one of them. You're grown up now but the enemy tried to make you afraid of the supernatural. God wants to break that fear off you and to ground your heart in love. If this is you, pray this prayer:

Father, in Jesus' name, I repent. I repent for not trusting you. I decide now to trust you to protect me. Lord, I will do everything I need to in order to keep my heart pure and walk in humility. Open my eyes to the supernatural around me. Take away all the associated fears so that I can enjoy supernatural encounters, visions, dreams, provision, and prophetic experiences. Lord, thank you for the angels, your ministering spirits sent to do your work and to partner with the saints. Holy Spirit, thank you for your discernment and guiding me toward the truth. Thank you, Lord, for launching me into a whole new level of experiences in your Kingdom, on this side of eternity. Amen.

CHAPTER FIVE

"Understanding Your Gift"

My first lesson in understanding the prophetic gift was taught by a man named John Paul Jackson, who has since gone home to be with the Lord. John Paul was a tremendous seer. I saw him minister quite a few times and it was always inspiring. He not only operated in amazing word of knowledge, he was also a dreamer and an interpreter of dreams. He even created an online school that equipped dreamers. I once watched as he ministered to a fellow supernatural student I knew. Although he was in supernatural school, he thought he was called to the business world. John Paul read the guy's mail like he knew him his whole life, like they were best friends. He told the guy, "You thought you were called to business, didn't you? But you've been called to ministry this whole time!" The guy had been studying the supernatural but failed to recognize and study his own giftings.

The Gifts Are Irrevocable

The gifts of the spirit aren't simply God moving through us, using us like puppets. They are gifts which, once given, belong to us. 1 Corinthians 14:1 says, "Pursue love, yet desire earnestly spiritual gifts, but especially that you may prophesy." Desire all the gifts, but *really* go after the prophetic. Romans 11:29 in the NASB says, "for the gifts and the calling of God are irrevocable." The King James puts it like this: "For the gifts and calling of God are without repentance." You can have a genuine gift of the Holy Spirit and operate in that gift without having a relationship with Jesus.

It's good to keep in mind that, when watching someone operate in a high-level gifting, it isn't necessarily because they have an intimate relationship with Jesus. What happens with many ministers, from God's generals to friends and mentors of mine, is we give our lives to Christ and there is an intense season in which we are wooed by the Holy Spirit. We spend hours and hours with the Lord Jesus, desperately hungry for Him. We learn to steward his presence and to hear his voice. We either learn about our gifts or use them in new, redeemed ways with pure emotions. Maybe God blesses your ministry and it grows as you become more and more recognized.

But then, the business of ministry begins to carve into our quiet time with God. You went from spending 20 hours a week minimum in the word to getting in a few minutes here and there. This is exactly what happened to me. By the time I was 20 I was thrust into full-time international ministry. I was traveling the world and had thousands attending my meetings. The power of God as tangible and people encountered the Holy Spirit in real ways. I almost went shopping for a white coat, thinking I was the next Benny Hinn. Although the ministry was genuine, during that season, I couldn't have been further away from Jesus.

The gifts are irrevocable. When I was starting out in ministry, I had little foundation in the word. I had about five messages, which is all a lot of itinerant ministers have, between three to five messages. God help them if the services extend or go into revival. I had my five messages memorized and I would just get up there and kind of rehash old manna, then at the end I would pray and prophesy. The more ministry invitations I got, the bigger my ego grew. I was prophesying over all types of people and because of where I was in my relationship with the Holy Spirit, I thought it all had something to do with me.

How many of you know God can speak through a donkey? That's exactly what I was, except more of the King James translation version of a donkey, if you know what I mean. Jesus said even the rocks will cry out (Luke 19:40)! God wasn't flowing through me because of how great a minister I was or because our relationship was rock-solid; it was because I was a willing vessel who would step out in faith to release the love of God to people.

I remember one meeting at which several of us ministered. I stood in the crowd while another man of God spoke and a woman stood in front of me. I watched as she leaned over to the man next to her and said, "I was in a car accident and I injured my L-5." Without asking her permission, a big no-no, I laid my hand on her back and prayed, "Father, I pray that you would just heal her L-5." She screamed and asked, "How did you know I injured my L-5?"

I said, "Well ma'am, I heard you tell the gentleman next to you."

She replied, "I didn't tell him anything. I don't even know him!" Turns out, I had an open vision so real I thought it happened in the natural. These kinds of experiences were happening when my relationship with Jesus suffered. I'd have dreams about meeting people, strangers, and the very next day I'd meet them. I thought Jesus and I were cool because my gift was operating so well. The reality was, I had gotten so enamored with the gifts that I'd forgotten all about the person of Jesus!

Do you find yourself worshiping Jesus only to get a word from him? If you're ministering, do you lead the service in worship only to then have a time of healing? A relationship with Jesus isn't a means to an end. If you worship him, healing follows. If you worship him, the prophetic breaks forth. What about just worshiping him because he's worthy and letting him do whatever he wants to do?

Galatians 3:5 says, "So then, does He who provides you with the Spirit and works miracles among you, do it by the works of the Law, or by hearing with faith?" Does he do it because you are perfectly holy? Does he do it because your character is intact? Does he do it because you have integrity? No! The scripture says that he works miracles among you because of your faith.

Stay Close to Jesus

That said, it can be dangerous to operate in your gift apart from Jesus. It's like running your car on an empty tank. Sooner or later, those fumes are going to run out and you'll end up on the side of the road. Our tanks go dry when we stop praying, stop soaking, stop spending time in the word. Eventually, we're no longer operating in the spirit, we're operating on adrenaline. I was addicted to adrenaline! There is a high that happens when you minister to people. I remember being invited to a meeting along with seven other young ministers. The host said, "God gave us each one of your names! We know your calling and what you're going to do with your lives." It was really encouraging, until he said, "The Lord had us pray for you because we saw each of you drinking coffee after coffee after coffee after coffee!" I had my latte in my hand. Every single one of us was an overseer. A few of the eight were overseeing international worship ministries. The host went on to say, "Some of you are no longer operating out of intimacy or the anointing of the Holy Spirit; you are operating out of caffeine and adrenaline. The Lord said if we didn't call you guys to rest you were going to be like shooting stars."

A year after I'd already been traveling internationally and my ministry was growing, I heard the Lord ask if I would attend Bethel School of Supernatural Ministry. A lot of people asked, "Why would you do that? You've already received the gifts of the Holy Spirit and you already have an itinerant ministry. You already have everything that they can give you." I knew the Holy Spirit was calling me there but I didn't know why. Early on Bobby Conner spoke to me and said, "Ivan, you've been asking the Lord 'why did you bring me here?' The Lord says because he wasn't going to let you be a rhinestone cowboy." As a Jersey boy, I had no clue what he was talking about. Bobby explained that there are real cowboys out there with these big belt buckles they win from riding bulls. They earn those things! Then there wannabe cowboys who go down to the Walmart and buy a big shiny belt buckle. The Lord didn't want me being one of the fakes.

Another prophet called me up another time and spoke over me, telling me things about myself I already knew. I thought to myself, *I know all this but I guess it's good they know who I am, too.* Then she said, "I see you like a boxer." I was boxing at the time so said, "Yep."

"I see you like a boxer and you step into the ring and the devil knocks you out!" I thought, *What a terrible word!* She went on to say that I wasn't ready to fight.

What? I prophesy really well. I heal the sick. I've seen blind eyes open! You want to see my resume? At the time, I was caught in this sort of one-upmanship that can go on between ministers behind the scenes. "I was in a meeting the other day and I prayed for somebody and a cyst about this big just fell right to the ground!"

Another minister would say, "That's amazing. I was in a meeting too, and a cyst fell that was *this big*!"

And a third would say, "That's great guys. I was in a meeting and a cyst the size of a basketball…" As if it were any of us causing the cysts to fall in the first place! That's the reason why the revivals of the 1940's and 1950's stopped: it became about whose tent was the biggest. It was about the ministers and their gifts. The Lord wanted me to avoid that trap so he began to establish in me an understanding of the Father's love. I didn't grow up in a Christian home so I had no understanding of a God who loved me. That's why I went to Bethel. During that season, God didn't take the gifts away from me because they're given without repentance. What he did was shift my mindset away from merely using a gift to build a ministry or platform to using my gift out of relationship with my best friend Jesus.

Bad theology says we have to make ourselves perfect before God can use us. If that were so they wouldn't be called gifts; they would have to be called rewards. I'm challenging the mentality that says, "Well, I don't know, young man. You just got saved. You shouldn't be moving in the gifts because you're not mature enough in the Lord."

[handwritten margin note: Contrast with it will take 15 to 20 years.]

I guess some people haven't read the bible where it says Jesus commissioned twelve untrained men as apostles. Jesus' way of ministry is very different than ours! You're probably aware that the church at Corinth had its problems, including a lack of love. Even so, the Lord allowed his Spirit to be poured out there. Why? So that they could better see the love they didn't have. When Paul brought correction he didn't say, "Look, you guys are the most spirit-filled church but you are missing it. What I need you to do is to totally stop prophecy, stop tongues, stop everything and just don't do it anymore until you've corrected your character." Yet this is exactly how some people approach the issue. What actually happens is that the power of

God exposes what's in someone's heart. So why deny someone the power of God?

If you want to see what is in somebody's heart, give them a leadership position. Few ways give you a window into someone's heart like leadership responsibility. Once you give them a little bit of authority, all the slag rises to the surface. Then what do you do? Do you say, "See! That's why I didn't want you in leadership in the first place!" No! What did Jesus do? When the disciples came back excited after being sent out and said, "Even the demons were subject to us in your name," did Jesus say, "Uh you guys! So young and immature. Give me those gifts back! I'll never let you use my giftings again; it's all about character you know!"

Jesus said, "I was watching Satan fall from heaven like lightning," Luke 10:18. He said, "I know! I saw what you did and it was awesome!" Before teaching them anything further, he patted them on the back, proud of what they'd done right. He did go on to admonish them not to "rejoice in this, that the spirits are subject to you, but rejoice that your names are recorded in heaven." He still gave them a lesson but his chief concern was rejoicing with them!

When my son prophesies over people, I don't say, "Well son, I don't want your identity getting wrapped up in your gift." Instead, I say, "Come here, little buddy! That's so amazing! I'm so proud of you! Don't forget, it's all about Jesus." That's what Jesus did. No rebuke, just a simple shift of their gaze to what's important.

If we act out of fear, we go to extremes. "Oh no! Don't forget about that one minister who fell from grace." Then we use that example to justify believing no one should be trusted with the gifts of the Holy Spirit. We need to understand there's a separation between the man and the move of God. Are you familiar with the Calvary Chapel and Vineyard movements? One of the central figures to both moves of God was a man named Lonnie Frisbee. If you haven't heard of Lonnie, it's because he was largely written out of the history of the Jesus People movement of the 1960s and 70s, or at least brushed to the side. Why? Because he struggled with homosexuality and died of AIDS. Here was a man with tremendous gifts: he was a seer prophet with incredible word of knowledge; and he was a power evangelist who moved in miracles, signs, and wonders. Lonnie's struggles had nothing to do with his gifting. God used him to bring thousands to Christ. He was a catalyst for one of the largest movements of the last hundred years. Unfortunately, after Lonnie's fall, many from the movement distanced themselves, not only from Lonnie but from demonstrations of the Spirit.

I sat once with a group of church leaders and confessed my disappointed with the current state of the Jesus People movement. They all fell silent. I tried to explain myself. "You know why I'm tired of it? I'm a student of church history and I've seen how God birthed this movement with signs and wonders and miracles and salvation and all of that! But now, it's like you can't see the fruit. It's almost like they have become Baptists!" I'm not getting down on Baptists, mind you. It's just they aren't known for moving in the power gifts. One of the leaders, a man who was well-connected to senior leadership of two of the largest movements impacted by the Jesus People, replied that he knew Lonnie Frisbee. I thought, *I'm about to get rebuked!*

He said, "I'll tell you what happened. They had the gifts of the Holy Spirit and the zeal for the Spirit of God—they just didn't know what to do with either. There was so much excess. So when it was revealed Lonnie was struggling with sin, they didn't know how to deal with that either. Basically, they decided that it was safer to shut it all down."

An entire generation witnessed the power of God and was invited to move in it, but they rejected it out of fear. Because of that, what you have now is new generation unfamiliar with the power of God. "For the Kingdom of God does not consist of words but in power," 1 Corinthians 4:20. Paul wrote to the church at Corinth in 1 Corinthians chapter two, "And when I came to you, brethren, I did not come with superiority of speech or of wisdom... And my message and my preaching were not in persuasive words of wisdom, but in demonstration of the Spirit and of power, so that your faith would not rest on the wisdom of men but on the power of God." Too much of the church rests its faith on the wisdom of men so that whenever someone talks about the supernatural, they say, "This is heresy!"

Can you imagine Jesus, when meeting someone in need of a healing, saying,

"Can somebody get this guy some Neosporin and an Advil?" No! Jesus exercised faith to heal out of love. It's the only thing that counts according to Galatians 5:6! He didn't offer words of condolences or medical wisdom, even though nothing is wrong with those. He offered something greater: his power! The supernatural gospel is not a new thing. This is New Covenant Christianity.

Has there been excess? Yes. Has it been misused? Yes. All that means is that you have to walk with Jesus all the more. Even closer. But don't swing the pendulum in the other direction. Don't over correct by denying the power. Figure out what your gifts are. Study your gift. Learn all you can about it, how it operates. Then practice it. Exercise it. And stay close to the one who gave it to you.

Mentoring

There's a scripture that really put the fear of God in me when I first read it. 2 Samuel 18:18 says, "Now Absalom in his lifetime had taken and set up for himself a pillar which is in the King's Valley, for he said, 'I have no son to preserve my name.' So he named the pillar after his own name, and it is called Absalom's Monument to this day." Absalom had no son so he built a monument to himself. What happens when we have giftings and anointings but we are not raising up the next generation? We put ourselves on platforms so that everybody can see us and say, "Ooh! Ah!"

Do you want to be a prophet? Who are you mentoring? "Oh, I don't believe I have to be a mentor in order to be a prophet." That's dangerous because that means it's all about you. You can't slow down enough to pour into the next generation? Even under the Old Covenant, they had the Sons of Prophets. We need to see generations walking alongside one another. We need to see a wiser generation walking with the younger, training them up, willing to call out bad and call up the good in them, always in love.

I was fortunate enough to serve with a pastor who was such an encouragement to my heart. I remember in one service I got up and I rebuked the church. I mean hard! I was young and I had heart issues. If your heart isn't good, you can still discern things in the realm of the spirit but it tends to be negative. You see the demonic everywhere. You see everything that doesn't align with God and scripture. That's what I did. I saw what the enemy was doing but not what the Father was saying to the church! So I got up and I just ripped the church apart. Then I went home and I had a dream. In the dream, I was sitting on a toilet in front of the entire congregation. You can figure out for yourself what that means. The Lord was correcting me. He then asked me if I would ever talk to my parents the way I spoke to the church. *No, Lord.* He reminded me of 1 Timothy 5:1, "Do not sharply rebuke an older man, but rather appeal to him as a father." *Lord, I'm so sorry!*

The next day I apologized to the senior pastor. He said, "I'm so proud of you." I was stunned. I felt I had just ruined his church! Why wasn't he angry?

"I'm so proud of you because you're a son. An illegitimate son doesn't receive discipline from his Father, but you have! The elders of the church wanted to bring you in for a speaking to. I convinced them instead to pray that God would speak to you last night himself." They prayed for me that God, my Father, would bring correction, then in a dream, he humbled my heart. The next Sunday, I stood before the congregation with tears in my eyes and I repented. Afterwards, people came forward to embrace me. It brought us so much closer together as a body.

One time, I was raising up this young seer prophet and ministered at a church where very few people attended. I mean there were like 12 people there. It was terrible! There had been some scandal that caused most to leave and it was basically just a bunch of friends who kept meeting together. After the service, the pastor approached and said, "I've never met anyone that sees stuff! Can you tell me, what kind of stuff do you see? Do you see angels? Do you see demons?"

The young guy I was mentoring said, "Oh yeah."

The pastor said, "Did you see any demons today at the service?" *Oh no.* I should have intervened right there. He said, "I saw lots of demons in the service!" I was in the backseat and I was trying to kick the chair and pull on the seatbelt, but he was so hard-headed that he was telling his story.

I was thinking, *Oh dear God! They're all friends!*

"Who did you see demons on?" She asked.

"You remember that woman with the pink shirt?" He said.

"Margaret?!?!"

I tapped him on the shoulder really hard and asked, "Hey, hey, hey! What was *the Lord* doing?" I had to get the conversation on track.

Some of you have grown up in cultures where you've tried to step out in your giftings, but because your character wasn't perfect or your theology wasn't perfect, you were smacked on the hand. Or you were pushed into a corner and shut down. Because of that, maybe you've embraced the same theology, perhaps without realizing it!

Sometimes religious folk, and even well-meaning people want to shy away from focusing on the gifts as if everything needs to be in perfect balance all the time. You say "hot," they say "cold," just to keep things even. I remember Bill Johnson said something to the effect of, "If I say 'we're sons of God,' someone else wants to say, 'Don't forget we're servants, too.'" Yes, that's true. And I absolutely value character over gifting. But it's possible to study and focus on particular aspects of the Christian life without inflating our egos or losing focus of what's most important. I do believe in balance, but what I don't believe in is a little hot, a little cold. That makes lukewarm. True balance is *all* of Jesus! I want *all* love and *all* faith flowing through me! I want all that Jesus died for on the cross.

If you're reading this and you have gray hair, you can testify to this: character isn't something you achieve by having hands laid on you. Character must be worked out through life. It's a process we all have to go through. The question is, are you patient enough? Are you enough of a father or mother to walk alongside somebody as they work through their process? I heard John Paul Jackson share a story from his youth when he interpreted an older minister's dream. The old man asked John Paul how he did it. "I don't know, I just do it," he replied.

The minister frowned and said, "That's very sad because when you die your gift dies with you." Because Absalom had no sons, he built a monument to himself. A monument may stand for a time, but its impact and reach are severely limited. Give me broken people over a perfect monument in stone any day. I want to walk with people in the midst of their brokenness and I want to see them shine like stars in the sky!

The way I love my wife and the way we express that love to each other is different from how couples express their love. Similarly, the Lord Jesus reveals his voice and love to each of us differently. We each have our own unique relationship with the Lord. I could never say, "This is exactly how to hear God." There are, however, some suggestions I can make to help you hear him for yourself. Some of that can be found in chapter three when I list different types of prophets. In reality, though, God can speak to you any way he chooses!

One thing I've learned to do is to yield my body unto righteousness. I actually pray Romans Six over myself and pray the blood of Jesus over my eye gate, my ears, over my heart, my hands, and my walk. Hebrews 5:14 says, "But solid food is for the mature, who because of practice have their senses trained to discern good and evil." Are your senses trained to discern good from evil? In the same way that you have physical senses, you also have spiritual senses according to Ephesians 1:17-19. "That the God of our Lord Jesus Christ, the Father of glory, may give to you a spirit of wisdom and of revelation in the knowledge of Him. I pray that the eyes of your heart may be enlightened, so that you will know what is the hope of His calling, what are the riches of the glory of His inheritance in the saints, and what is the surpassing greatness of His power toward us who believe. These are in accordance with the working of the strength of His might."

Spiritual Senses

You might not be a seer prophet but if you're born again, you can see the Kingdom of God. In John 3:5, Jesus says to Nicodemus, "Truly, I say to you, unless one is born of water and the Spirit he cannot enter into the kingdom of God." But two verses earlier, Jesus said almost the same thing with a slight change: "Truly, I say to you, unless one is born again he cannot see the kingdom of God." Catch the difference? Jesus made a distinction between *entering* the Kingdom and *seeing* the Kingdom. The challenge is that most of us have entered the kingdom but we're not seeing the kingdom! Reading this passage in the Amplified Bible, it connects seeing with experiencing. If you're born again, you have a new set of eyes in your heart with which you can see and experience the Kingdom of God! It's what was promised in Joel 2:28-29: "It will come about after this that I will pour out My Spirit on all mankind; and your sons and daughters will prophesy, your old men will dream dreams, your young men will see visions. Even on the male and female servants I will pour out My Spirit in those days."

You've got spiritual senses, but how do you use them? Faith. Expect to see things. Early in my ministry, I looked like a madman during worship because I was also scanning the room, looking. People would come up to me and tell me to "calm down, just worship." Maybe I looked nervous. But I'd read in Habakkuk chapter two that Habakkuk would "keep watch to see what He will speak to me." By faith, I was looking. Guess what happened? I saw! I was preaching one service when suddenly half of the room was bathed in the color red. Then, the color blue swept into the other side. I then watched as the colors collided into a beautiful purple. It wasn't until after the service that the Lord revealed the meaning: the red was the blood of Jesus, the blue was revelation, and when mixed, they release royal authority. But I only saw because I was looking.

Some people say, "Well if God wants to show me something, he can show me." Sure, you can wait around for God to show you something unexpected. Me? I'm appropriating by faith! I believe with everything in me that God loves his people so much that he wants to speak to them, so I look every day for what he will say.

That being said, there will be seasons in which you see more, and seasons you see less. It's the same with dreams, visions, etc. Sometimes it may just be the still small voice for months at a time. If you feel like you're in a season where you're not hearing God like you used to, maybe he changed the frequency on the radio to get you out of your comfort zone. He's a jealous God; he likes to be pursued.

There's not just seeing in the spirit but there's also smelling. And tasting, and hearing. Now I know that might sound strange but I remember getting invited to pray for somebody in the hospital. Right away, I had this foul taste in my mouth. I thought, *What is that? It's disgusting!* When I got to the hospital, I asked the patient what was wrong and he told me he had cancer. Immediately I knew, I'd tasted cancer! Before I had even walked into the hospital! Now I'm not saying that every person with cancer has a demon, but with this particular person, it was a spirit of death. Soon after, whenever I was invited to pray for someone, I was able to say, "Don't tell me what you have. I'm going to tell you." I'd learned how to discern through tasting in the spirit.

How Does God Speak To You?

Don't limit the Holy Spirit in the way that he wants to speak to you. And don't compare how he speaks to you with how he speaks to others. With me, I feel like God has to say, "Boy! I'm talking to you!" There are some of you with whom he doesn't have to yell because your ear is so inclined to his heart that he can whisper. Some people see more than they hear. Others hear more than they feel. Others discern more than they see. What's the best and most accurate way to hear from God? In the manner he chooses to talk to you.

When I was a ministry intern, I once walked into a pastor's office to get the speaker for the night. I found him on his hands and knees, hair disheveled, and face red. I was worried he had a heart attack! He said, "I just had an angelic encounter!" I escorted him to the service where, during worship, I told him I believed I'd gotten a word, too. "What is it?" He asked.

I told him what I heard but I was unsure of myself. I couldn't say that I'd heard it distinctly. An angel certainly hadn't brought it to me. It seemed more a thought than anything. Still, I told him.

He said, "That's exactly the word the angel brought me!"

I was worried because my revelation wasn't delivered in an encounter and therefore couldn't be as important. When we compare ourselves to others, it can make us feel less gifted. But we're the body of Christ! We can't all be the elbow, or the eye, or the nose! We all operate differently.

For some of you, you've grown up with such a relationship with Jesus that his thoughts are your thoughts. I've traveled all over the world teaching on hearing the voice of God then do these activations. I'd say, "Ask the Lord this question and raise your hand if God spoke to you." All the right-brained people would raise their hands. I had no breakthrough with the engineers, mathematicians, and scientists, though. *God, what's going on?* The Lord took me back to Habakkuk 2:1-3. "I will stand on my guard post and station myself on the rampart; and I will keep watch to see what He will speak to me, and how I may reply when I am reproved. Then the Lord answered me and said, 'Record the vision and inscribe it on tablets, that the one who reads it may run. For the vision is yet for the appointed time; it hastens toward the goal and it will not fail. Though it tarries, wait for it; for it will certainly come, it will not delay.'" I learned that the act of journaling occupies the left side of the brain, allowing creativity to flow. I started doing journaling exercises in my activations and enjoyed 100% success.

One of the clearest ways to hear the voice of God is to listen to what he put in your heart. Ezekiel 36:26-27 says, "Moreover, I will give you a new heart and put a new spirit within you; and I will remove the heart of stone from your flesh and give you a heart of flesh. I will put My Spirit within you and cause you to walk in My statutes, and you will be careful to observe My ordinances."

"What about Jeremiah 17," some of you might ask. "The heart is more deceitful than all else and is desperately sick; who can understand it?" Go back a couple verses and see that Jeremiah 17 talks about "the sin of Judah." You're not Judah! Jeremiah 17:1 says, "The sin of Judah is written down with an iron stylus; with a diamond point it is engraved upon the tablet of their heart…" That's the number one historical-contextual hermeneutic: figure out who the original audience was. Don't forget, that original audience was under the law. Ezekiel 36, on the other hand, prophesies what will happen under the New Covenant: You'll get a new heart and it will cause you to obey!

If you feel like you don't hear God, you may be caught up in your mind. Write down what you *think* the Lord is saying to you. Maybe his voice sounds like your own thoughts and you've been ignoring him this whole time. Learn to discern by writing it down. The more you practice, the better you'll hear. The more you expect, the more amazing things will happen!

Maybe you don't hear God because you don't ask him anything. Don't forget to ask questions! If you're going to Starbucks, take a moment and ask if there's anyone there he wants you to speak to. Maybe you get an image in your mind of a red plaid shirt. Don't leave it there. Ask God for a name. If you don't hear a name, that's okay. Whatever you do, don't give up and decide God doesn't want to talk to you. Remember: God is relational. Try asking a different question. "Is it a man or a woman, Jesus? What do you want to say to this person?" Keep pressing. Expect God to talk with you. But don't expect to know *everything*. He still wants you to step out in faith.

If you don't hear God, it's also possible you're asking too much, too loudly. Patricia King tells a story about how she fasted and prayed and contended for a word for the New Year. After hearing nothing, she eventually grew exhausted and laid down to rest. That's when she heard God say, "Finally! You're quiet! Now I can answer." Psalm 46:10 says, "Cease striving and know that I am God."

I sat next to a woman on an airplane once who was reading a book titled *The Celestine Prophecy*. I saw the word "prophecy" and thought, *This is going to be a fun ride*. I love those opportunities because they're trapped next to me the whole flight! I asked what the book was about and we had a friendly conversation. Meanwhile, I was thinking, *Oh Lord! What do you want to say to this woman?* "Tell her she's writing a book." In my mind, I even saw the chapter title *Talking to the Wind*.

I said, "Excuse me, ma'am, I don't mean to interrupt you, but are you writing a book?" She gasped and asked how I knew. We kept talking and she revealed she'd been raised in the church but there had been abuse so she turned her back. The Lord healed her heart there on that plane and she gave her life back to Jesus. All because I knew she was writing a book. I didn't even tell her everything God told me about her! So often in the church, you have to tell somebody their name, their birthday, their mama's name, what they had for breakfast, and they still want more. "Let's see if you have another word that's better than the last word I received." But those in the world, they're so open! Practice your gift.

Earnestly seek and desire the spiritual gifts, 1 Corinthians 14:1. The word for "seek and desire" is zéloó. It means to *covet* or to *lust after*. Pursue love first and always! But seek these gifts because they are empowerments that bring breakthrough and healing to people's hearts.

Some of you are psalmists and you need to sing over people! Now that might be a little strange if you were to just walk up to somebody you don't know and sing a song over them, but hey, why not? However the Lord leads. With that being said, I do tend to deliver words differently in the church versus out in the world. If you walk up to somebody from the world and you say, "I have a word for you. The Lord says he wants you to crucify the old man," they might think you've given permission for them to murder their husband!

"I see you have an anointing on your life."

"I'm annoying? God says I'm annoying?"

There's a language, a way of speaking we're familiar with in the church. Outside the church? You can sound like a crazy person. Leave the Christianese in the church. We have to learn how to communicate in a way people will understand.

Learn How Your Gift Operates

Early on, my timing was terrible. I assumed every word the Lord gave me was for that exact moment. I felt it would happen *right now*! I'd receive revelation, run to find my wife, excitedly share it with her, then we'd sit back and wait for it to happen. And wait. A week would go by. Then a month, a year, two years. Finally, it would come to pass. I had to learn that God sometimes told me things way before they happened. Those early years were rough. About two years after I'd started my itinerant ministry and flopped, I began receiving phones calls. "Remember that prophetic word you gave me way back?"

"Oh. Yeah. Sorry about that," I'd say.

"Why are you apologizing? It happened exactly the way you said it would! We had just about lost hope it would ever come to pass." *Really? Me too.* It was so embarrassing, giving words and seeing so little fruit. It turns out, many of those words did come to pass. It just took longer than I wanted them too. Then I realized my wife's gifting complimented my own. She walks in word of wisdom and often carried the timing element to revelation I received. I'd have vivid, incredibly realistic encounters and be convinced the what I saw was going to happen immediately. But my wife would step in and say, "Honey, that's not for now." What I'd forgotten was, very early in my ministry, a man told me this would happen. "The Lord is going to use your wife as a timing piece for you."

Pffft! What does she know? I thought I knew everything. I thought God would tell me everything I needed to know. I was so arrogant. Now, when I have these intense experiences, the first person I go to is my wife. "Babe, what do you think about this?"

"It's not now."

"It's the Lord!"

"But it is not now."

Accountability in the prophetic is a good thing. Don't be afraid to ask people how words you've given them have worked out. And don't be afraid of others asking you the same. If it turns out you missed a word, don't worry. Apologize, repent, and stay close to Jesus. I don't mean apologize and forget. Repent means to figure out why you might have missed it and then realign yourself with the mind of Christ. Can you imagine the healing that could happen within the church if prophetic people would actually apologize for missed words instead of just removing them from their websites when they don't happen? How many times has the end of the world been prophesied? Whatever happened to Y2K? On January 1st, 2000, none of those doomsday prophecies could be found. There is no accountability that way! Accountability comes through relationship. Mentor and be mentored. Find your spiritual mom and dad or get a group of trusted friends around you with whom you can share deeply personal prophetic words. Not only will they keep you accountable, they can help you study your gift. They may notice that most of your prophetic words of late don't come to pass until about three or six months out. They can point out if God is doing something new in your ministry. You'll be able to minister with greater clarity, which benefits you and those you minister to.

Giving personal prophetic words is one of the easiest ways to minister. The person is in front of you and you can close your eyes and pray over them and the Holy Spirit speaks. Corporate words, however, are a bit more challenging. If you're traveling to a church and the Lord speaks to you what he's doing in that region, write it down. Pray about it and ask the Holy Spirit what he wants you to do with the information.

I had a dream one time about this particular place in Washington. I was given all sorts of revelation but I thought, *I'm never going to get invited there.* Then, I was sitting in an airplane with my wife and next to us was a girl who lived in that same part of Washington! The word wasn't for me to give to the region, it was for her!

Pay attention and be a good steward with the revelation God gives you. The best way to be a good steward is to study your gift. Figure out how it operates. If you're a seer, how do you see? In the natural or the spirit? When do you see? At night, at breakfast, in the shower? Do you see more in your prayer closet or during a worship service? If you're a dreamer, are you writing down your dreams? Do you dream prophetically at night or during naps in the day? Are your dreams realistic or symbolic? If symbolic, do you keep track of which symbols consistently mean what to you? It's your responsibility to learn how your gift operates.

Honor the gift. Respect it. Paul Cain made a habit of writing down prophetic words in a journal. Whenever something he prophesied came to pass, he could open his journal and point to the day God gave him that revelation. He didn't just get a word, share it, then forget it. He honored every word the Lord gave him. So should we!

CHAPTER SIX

"The Gift of Prophecy and the Office of a Prophet"

When it comes to the prophetic, I might be asked this question more than any other: what's the difference between the gift of prophecy and the office of a prophet?

It's not a business card and a website. It's how each operates in the body of Christ.

The gifts in 1 Corinthians 12 are gifts given by the spirit. Faith, healing, miracles, prophecy... He freely gives as he wills. They are his gifts to you. The Ephesians 4 gifts, on the other hand, teachers, pastors, evangelists, apostles, and prophets, are themselves the gifts to the church. The first instance speaks of *having* a gift while the second speaks of *being* a gift. A believer may possess the gift of prophecy, but the church is blessed by the gift of a prophet.

For a decade now, I've been teaching what is essentially Prophetic 101. This is where people get activated in the prophetic, where they learn everyone can prophesy, their faith gets stirred up and they take their first steps in the prophetic. For an office prophet, it's not so much learning how to turn the gift on, as it is learning how to turn it off!

If you have the gift of prophecy, you operate your gift. On your way to minister at a church, you're speaking in tongues, stirring your spirit, asking God "what do you want to say to this church today?" At the meeting, you deliver your message and give a few people encouraging words. Praise God! We should all be doing that! If you're an office prophet, there's no need to stir up your spirit in order to get the gift working. You walk into the building and Now with the function of the prophet, it's not stirring it up with tongues. Sure, you can pray in into an open vision. I was in Hawaii once, just walking to the bathroom when I walked past a woman. I had a vision of a massive tsunami and fish falling on the shore. I said, "Excuse me, listen, I don't know anything about your family but I feel like many of your family members are not saved and they're from a different country. I see this massive wave and it is bringing the harvest of your family." She looked at me and started to cry.

She said, "I was just on the phone with my family. Many of them are not saved! But they're finally beginning to be open to what I have to say."

I didn't have to pray in tongues. I was just walking. As a prophet, you're always "on." You shake somebody's hand and immediately see their sin like a banner over their head. It's challenging! For those with a gift of prophecy, you don't generally see angels all the time or walk headlong into open visions on your way to the bathroom. One person exercises a gift. The other is hardwired to receive revelation.

Someone with the gift of prophecy carries a bowl of the oil of anointing and uses it a little at a time. An office prophet is dunked head first into a vat of oil and drips it wherever they go.

Just recently on a flight back from Germany, a woman sat next to me. She sat uncomfortably close and was being a little too friendly. I was tired and trying to avoid her. She asked what I did for a living. "I'm a pastor." That usually shuts them down.

"Oh, that's awesome! What were you doing in Germany?" I told her I had just preached at a conference. "Wonderful! Do you mind if I ask what the topic was?"

I thought, *This'll scare her*. "It was a prophetic conference. I taught something called the School of the Prophets."

"Tell me everything!" She was so hungry that she pulled School of the Prophets out of me! I taught her everything, breaking it all down right there on the plane. Then the prophetic invaded the teaching.

"Hypothetically speaking, let's say you have a family member struggling with heroin addiction."

"My sister's boyfriend is addicted to heroin."

"Let's just pretend that you go to a Baptist church."

"My hairs are standing up on end. I go to a Baptist church." That's how it went with all my examples.

"Let's just pretend for a minute that when you were very young you had all of these supernatural experiences. You'd get up in the middle of the night, run to your mom and dad, and they'd say, 'Oh honey there's no boogie monster under your bed. Just go to sleep.'" She nodded so I said, "And let's just say that you continued to have this hunger for the supernatural all through high school then all of the sudden you began to pursue some form of witchcraft."

"I pursued Wicca," she said.

It was just a conversation! I wasn't even trying to be prophetic! But, the gift of a prophet is in the communication. You talk and sometimes God speaks through you. This woman had a hunger for the supernatural her entire life. She'd had visions, encounters, she'd had dreams that came to pass, but there was no place in the church for her. So, she pursued new age beliefs and got answers for her gifting there. When she decided it was time to settle down, get married, and have a family, she put herself in the Baptist church. There, all of the stuff she'd experienced, all the supernatural, she started to believe it had been demonic and left it all behind in her past.

Goodness! Do you know how many people in the church—or who aren't in church anymore—are actually prophets of God?

Matthew 10:41 says, "He who receives a prophet in the name of a prophet shall receive a prophet's reward; and he who receives a righteous man in the name of a righteous man shall receive a righteous man's reward." What is the prophet's reward? Eyes to see and ears to hear. In whatever way you receive a minister, that's what you'll reap. In places where I've been introduced as an evangelist, no matter how much I minister in the prophetic, there will still be people in the audience who only reap evangelism. Not a bad thing! But in places that receive me as a prophet, they begin to pull on me in the spirit and the prophetic flows out with ease. Their reward is the word of God for their lives and region.

I've ministered in places where it was obvious they had no idea why they'd invited me. They weren't pulling on me for anything. So, for lack of anything else, I'd teach. I did that in order to create relationship and trust. I'd teach on the prophetic which motivated them to pull the prophetic out of me. The Lord used me to introduce the prophetic, both the gift and the office, to those bodies.

Because of the way a lot of us have done church, especially in the more charismatic circles, we often believe the person with the microphone declaring the word of God every Sunday is the prophet of the church. Not necessarily. Prophets aren't necessarily the ones traveling and ministering at conferences. These are often people with high-level gifts of prophecy. An office prophet, in reality, is the one who has the ear of the apostolic minister. She's second in charge next to the apostle who leads the direction of the church. A true five-fold prophet isn't zealous to get up and grab the microphone just prophesy anytime he wants to because she knows words have to be weighed, judged, and tested.

Sometimes, the judging process at a church lacks. Prophets are black and white - what they see is what it is! They're wired for justice. Churches with prophets but no apostolic leaders can be dangerous for everybody. The prophet can be less of a help and more of a wrecking ball. Without guidance and direction, people often don't know what to do with prophetic revelation. This can alienate the prophet, wounding them. Words they've given, even if true, can be thought of as wrong. They stop walking in love and kindness, as does the church because they're hurt by the words meant to help.

The same hurt can sometimes be caused by the title of prophet being bestowed too early on immature believers. They might actually be prophets but the title can easily go to their heads if they're not ready. I have prophet friends who are careful with the kinds of stories they share with young prophets. They hold back on stories about ministering to governments and kings so that those encounters won't replace Jesus as their focus. Instead, their identities should be found in sonship. A son or a daughter can function in a church where a prophet has caused harm in the past.

For people eager to give a word at all times, that can be a sign of either a gift of prophecy or an immature prophet. The longer you operate in a prophetic ministry, the more you begin to pray, "Lord, if you really want me to share this, you've got confirm it to me." Like I've said, not everything God tells you is necessary to be shared. I walked into a particular church and saw a wineskin in the spirit realm. The Lord said, "I only pour new wine into new wineskins. I'm going to shift the entire leadership of this church and many in the eldership will be transitioned." With the zeal of a young man I went up to the pastor and I said, "Listen, here is what's about to happen…" The eldership team were his friends of over 20 years! He'd even attended elementary school with one of them. As you can imagine, he didn't receive the word very well. Or me for that matter. A short while later, some of the leadership told him their plans to transition out. The revelation was true but had I been more mature, I might not have shared it.

Occasionally confused with the gift of the prophetic is word of knowledge. They are two different things. A word of knowledge is information about someone's past or present. It might be a name, an address, a medical condition, discerning of spirits, etc. The gift of prophecy begins to predict events yet to come, to reveal God's heart and plans for someone's future.

I've been invited on many occasions to visit a church, ministry, or business and to "get a feel" for what's going on. "Would you pace the hallways of our offices? Would you spend some time with our leadership like an undercover agent and give us feedback about what you discern?" Word of knowledge might reveal, "I saw a lot of wounded hearts that need a father's love." The gift of prophecy might show, "The Lord is raising this team up and bringing a mighty breakthrough!" But a prophet would walk in and say, "You know that one guy? Your vice president? If you don't get him into a position of less authority, his ambition for something separate is going to split this ministry." That last one isn't a word you'd want to declare in front of everyone.

Bill Johnson once told me, "We can't make any decisions in our church without God telling the prophets here first." Amos 3:7 says, "Surely the Lord God does nothing unless He reveals His secret counsel to His servants the prophets." That's part of the prophet's platform. You may have a gift that's in operation and it comes in seasons or waves, but what's the platform, favor, and influence God has given you?

You may have a very specific prophetic word when all of the sudden you hear of a prophet delivering the exact same word to the President. You say, "Well I heard that!" You probably did. But you didn't have the favor, platform, or influence to give it. That's something else which separates prophets from the gift of prophecy. If you're an office prophet, God will increase your platform until you find yourself with influential connections. You'll have relationships in government, open doors to speak to politicians, policy makers, and CEOs of large companies. Then, when you get a word, you're able to deliver it. Bobby Conner tells a story about how the government offered to put a red phone in his home with a direct line to the CIA. He turned it down because it was too much paperwork but the point is his platform was visible enough that even the CIA wanted to know what Bobby knew!

Mantles vs. Anointings

I wrote briefly before about a church that used me like an attack dog. I was brought on board as a part of the eldership to call out the sin and error in people the church had a problem with. Back then, I was too immature to know what needed to be said, and what needed to be withheld. Instead, if I saw it, I said it. That's what I was brought on board to do. But the public reason was they wanted a prophet to aid them in a time of transition. Actually, the revelation I shared with them is what caused a lot of the leadership to transition out.

Eventually, the leadership who stayed, who welcomed me with open arms and who used my gift to keep the church in line, got a taste of their own medicine. They had plans to build an apostolic team but I told them it would be impossible. "None of you are apostolic." They didn't like hearing that. They started having secret meetings to which I wasn't invited. Instead of working with me, mentoring me, helping me to lose my rough edges and encourage the church, they rejected me. I was a loose cannon that needed put in a corner. It's an all-too familiar story when it comes to prophets.

The corner they put me in was youth ministry. I went from a prophet to a youth pastor, except I was still a prophet. Prophets aren't meant to pastor! Continually calling people out on their stuff is no way to grow a church! Confrontation can be good for growth but it doesn't fill the pews. Jesus had his 12 disciples who laid down their lives. Then there was the 70, who were sent out into ministry but they didn't inherit the church; the 12 did. Then there was the crowd who only came to be fed. The crowd are those who got offended and jumped ship. But the 12, those you can depend on. The prophet exposes the 70 from the crowd and the 12 from the 70. A prophet's ministry will usually have a few die-hard fans but huge numbers don't hang on.

When I found myself the new youth pastor, I asked God why I was in that situation. Then I saw a mantle floating in the spirit. I asked him what it was. "Put it on." So I did: it was a pastor's mantle. There was an assignment given to me to pastor the youth, and I was given the grace to do just that. There's a difference between your calling, what you're anointed to do, and a mantle. Mantles are given when you are assigned a mission. When God commissions his leaders like Joshua he releases mantles over them which gives them the supernatural ability to complete their missions. Unlike the gifts and calls that remain on a person throughout life, a mantle stays with the mission and not with the man.

Joseph is given a coat of many colors from his father. That coat represented favor but it also represented leadership. He was called as a prophet—he dreamed and interpreted dreams. But he was mantled for leadership, among his family and later in Egypt. In Potiphar's house, he was given a new robe to put on as the head servant: another mantle! People can have multiple mantles in their lifetime but their calling and gifting don't change.

I've heard people complain, "I used to pastor a church. I had a gift of healing and operated in word of knowledge. Then God called me to business and I'm no longer in ministry." If you were once called to be a pastor, you're always called. Just because the Lord shift you to business doesn't mean you retire as a pastor. You can't retire your function in the body. A hand can't stop being a hand. It can, however, stop using a pen and use a plow instead. A pastor, like a prophet, is a five-fold ministry calling. God calls the five-fold. You can ask God for the gifts and operate in different gifts, but you do not pray and fast to be an apostle. "Paul, an apostle, called by the will of God." It's the same thing with Jeremiah. "Before I formed you in the womb I knew you, and before you were born I consecrated you; I have appointed you a prophet to the nations," Jeremiah 1:5.

Now, this hypothetical pastor is in business and thinks to himself, *How have I failed God?* He needs to recognize that business isn't a demotion but rather a mantle God has given him for a season. There is an anointing on him to fulfill an assignment and something in that assignment will help him graduate to where God wants to take him.

I was once in a season of working a day job. I'm not above working any job, in fact, I like working. I was already operating as a prophet at the time, and my employers knew I was a minister, and they asked that I keep that stuff to myself. They respected my faith, they just didn't want me preaching to them. "No worries!," I told them. I was good with that. Next thing you know, I was having dreams about the business. I didn't have a platform or a microphone, it was as simple as asking for a few minutes to talk with my boss. He liked what I had to say and wanted to hear more!

Some of us are so "churchy" we think we have to be in a position of church leadership to be a prophet! That's old wineskin thinking. God is trying to break us out of that mold! Learn to function in who you are, everywhere you are. You don't need a title! After a while at that job, they started asking me questions like, "What do you see for me? What does God see for me?" I didn't have to preach to them. Regardless, during that season, I wasn't mature enough yet to feel like a prophet even though I was operating as one because I was working a menial job. But it's in those seasons you get promoted. Servanthood positions you for the mantle God has for you.

The Gift of Prophecy and the Office of a Prophet

1 Kings 19:19 says, "So he departed from there and found Elisha the son of Shaphat, while he was plowing with twelve pairs of oxen before him, and he with the twelfth. And Elijah passed over to him and threw his mantle on him." Elisha was a hard working man! It doesn't say that Elijah found Elisha on his couch. It's called the work of the ministry. Twelve oxen also represent that he was a wealthy man. He didn't need to do the plowing himself. And Elijah, he had just been hiding in a cave from Jezebel. Strange that a man who'd just had a power encounter—he'd just seen the fire of God slay 300 prophets of Baal—would be scared of any death threat. He was so broken and afraid, God had to say to him "I need you to go anoint this one guy as king and this other guy as a prophet in your stead." So Elijah gave Elisha his mantle then Elisha asked to go home and kiss his parents goodbye before following. Elijah's response was, "What have I don't to you? You're going to experience the same stuff I've had to experience. What have I done to you? Of course, go see your parents." Not only does Elisha go to kiss mom and dad, but he slaughtered the oxen! He burned his Plan B to the ground!

Luke 9:62 says, "But Jesus said to him, "No one, after putting his hand to the plow and looking back, is fit for the kingdom of God." Matthew 16:24 says, "Then Jesus said to His disciples, "If anyone wishes to come after Me, he must deny himself, and take up his cross and follow Me."

2 Kings 3:11 says that Elisha washed Elijah's hands. It's important today to wash your hands before you eat but it was way more important back then. They didn't have toilet paper. It was Elisha's job to wash Elijah's hands. That doesn't sound like fame or super-stardom. That's servanthood. Then Elisha asked the unthinkable: "I want a double portion of your mantle." If this were one of our charismatic meetings, it'd go like this: "Praise God! Wham! Bam! Everybody receives a double portion! I'm going to give you double of what I don't even have! You want an anointing to raise the dead? I've never raised the dead, but here, take it!" I'm not trying to make fun, I just want to make a distinction. Elijah had a better response. "You've asked a very hard thing! But keep your eyes on me. If you can stay focused, if you can keep your eyes on me then you'll get it in the end."

Before that, Elijah tried to shake Elisha in Gilgal, which prophetically speaks of circumcision or the removal of the flesh. No wonder Elisha didn't want to stay. 2 Kings 2:2 says, "Elijah said to Elisha, "Stay here please, for the Lord has sent me as far as Bethel." But Elisha said, "As the Lord lives and as you yourself live, I will not leave you." Bethel was the place where Jacob rested his head and he saw the angels of God ascending and descending—open heavens. Again Elisha wouldn't stay put. From there they traveled to Jericho, where Joshua and his army walked around the city, shouting and blowing trumpets until the walls came down—city transformation. And again, Elisha wouldn't stay. He wasn't satisfied with past moves of God. He knew he was called to more.

Prophets, arise! Get stirred up again! Don't let depression or complacency hinder you. Don't let one good experience satisfy your hunger. Prophets are called as change-agents to the church. If you're complacent, you're no longer roaring. Don't let anyone take your roar! If you're trying to be mean then cut it out, but if you are being you then be you! There was a part of Jesus that offended people. If you're speaking the truth in love and it still offends people, then what are you going to do? Walk around apologizing to everyone? No! Some of us are wired this way by God!

From Jericho, Elijah and Elisha crossed the Jordan river—a literal and metaphorical crossing over into the promises of God. You would think the guy would have earned the mantle by then. Instead, a chariot of fire arrived! That would be pretty distracting. No one would blame him for missing the whirlwind that took Elijah. But Elisha didn't miss it. He cried out, "My father, my father!" I believe the first "father" referred to Elijah, his spiritual father but the second was because he caught a glimpse of God! He ripped apart his old clothes, took up the mantle of Elijah, and smacked the river with it. "Where is the Lord, the God of Elijah?" Whoosh! The waters split and he crossed, walking in his new mantle.

There will be many distractions, disappointments, discouragements, rejections, isolation, hurt, and wounds to hinder you from walking in the fullness of your calling. You can give up, stay at Bethel or Jordan or Jericho or Gilgal. But something is built into the life of a prophet. They don't give up easily. We have to get to a place where we are not just focused on the angelic and the wonders of the supernatural but on

Abba Father. At that point, security and sonship comes and changes everything! It's a process, and often a difficult one.

One of the testimonies I hear the most from people called to the office of prophet is this: "God called me! It was amazing. I had an angelic experience," or, "I had a dream," or, "I went to a meeting and somebody called me out as a prophet."

"And then what happened?"

"All hell broke loose! It was terrible!" Yeah, that sounds about right. Psalm 105:19 says that the word of the Lord tried Joseph. Are you going to contend? Are you going to fight for this thing? Are you going to believe for this thing?

The Prophet has to exhort the church. Oftentimes the prophet will go through things before the body goes through things so that the prophet can say, "I know what you're experiencing but there's hope on the other side." There are suffering and difficulties that are all worth it in the end.

Avoid unnecessary suffering by waiting for God's appointment to establish your mantle. Elisha was appointed by God as a prophet to succeed Elijah but God used Elijah to recognize, prepare, and establish that appointment. God uses those in oversight and authority to recognize and establish us in our calling at the right time. All the words I received that I was a prophet were from well-established, credible, prophetic people. If you are fighting and striving to get a position, then you're trying to skip the process.

Being called by God is the easy part. The hard part is the training. This phase is sometimes called the PIT: Prophet-in-Training. For this reason, most if not all prophets need inner healing. Part of that healing comes when the body acknowledges the need for the whole five-fold ministry. This is mostly a problem in western churches, as I've touched on before. In other countries, you meet an apostle and ask, "What makes you an apostle?

"Jesus came to me and told me so."

"What's the fruit?"

"I have 5,000 churches and I have raised 12 people from the dead."

"Well all right then!"

Meanwhile, in America, we're still asking, "Are tongues real? Can women even minister?"

And don't be discouraged by the noise on the Internet. This new apostolic-prophetic movement we're in gets a lot of flak online. You know what? Martin Luther caught the same flak. After he nailed his 95 Theses to the church door, he was called a madman and a heretic. All he said was what the Bible said! "It's the priesthood of all believers! The Bible, the written word of God, is the final authority, not the Pope!" All of the sudden there was a Protestant Reformation and we are Protestants today because of a prophet who received a revelation from God and shouted it from the rooftops.

Don't have misconceptions: it's hard to be a prophet. It's hard because God will speak things to you people don't want to embrace. Ask John the Baptist. Messages aren't always received. But you've got to be tenacious in order to persevere.

Don't fail to also be humble. Humility is beautiful. Learning to use our gifts in conjunction with humility is when God releases you. It doesn't happen overnight, and don't fake it! That's trying to skip the process. It was hard for me at first because my identity was wrapped up in it. Now, God will say to me, "Do you see that person there?"

"Yes, Lord."

"Go whisper this..." I walk over and quietly whisper a word to them then they fall on the ground crying while I sneak away. It's not about me! God just wanted to encounter that person. Then you have the immature or wounded prophets: "Nobody ever listens to me!" Meanwhile, they're reaching for the microphone. But when we allow God to establish us there is a brokenness, humility, and grace that flows so freely!

Don't be afraid of the process. Don't be afraid of scars. After a long journey, it's likely you'll walk with a limp. Trust that. Scars mean you've been through process. It means you've earned your mantle or mantles. You're someone God can trust with his secrets.

CHAPTER SEVEN

"Different Characteristics of Prophets"

We're all aware that no two people are alike but when it comes to the function of a prophet, I've discovered that, although prophets all operate differently they share similar characteristics. They have similar passions, similar things they love and similar things they hate. I want to lay out some of the characteristics of a prophet to bring more clarity and so that you're better able to identify yourself as one. It's my experience that prophets struggle with themselves. They struggle with insecurity and with the call of God on their lives. My heart is to call out the gold from prophets, to see them healed and operate to their fullest.

Prophets are Agents of Change

Prophets are called to bring reformation. Scripture calls John the Baptist a prophet despite his only message being "repent and prepare the way of the Lord." Repentance comes from the Greek word *metanoia* which means to change the way you think. John's ministry, his mission, was to prepare the way for the reformation Jesus was to bring. His message was one for the future; both the immediate future and beyond.

It takes a Samuel to see David as the future king while he is just a boy. It takes an Elijah to see Elisha, a farmer, but will one day rise up to take his place as a prophet. It takes an Ezekiel to call a valley of dry bones an army. Not only are these visions of the future, they are also drastic changes. Prophets are wired for change. And not everybody is comfortable with change.

For this reason, prophets can seem really annoying to the rest of the church. Take Noah for example. "It's going to rain!" It had never rained up until that point before. People had never seen it, didn't know what it was. Then here's this wacko talking about rain, whatever that is, and building an ark because a flood is coming! His neighbors see the poor guy and say, "What possible use could we have for that thing? He's saying something's about to happen that has *literally never happened.*"

But Noah had a word from the Lord. That's the journey of a prophet: knowing God's plan for a person or region and then struggling with getting others on board. It's like prophesying revival to people who have no context for it. "Revival. That sounds fun." Instead of, "Yes God! How can I align my heart and my lifestyle for what you're going to do?"

Once I had a dream where I was running around to people in their beds and I was saying, "Wake up! The time is now! Wake up! The time is now! Awake! The time has come!" So much of the function of the prophet is in-your-face, saying, "Wake up, people!" Not everyone likes that. If the prophet brings a word of preparation, people often don't get excited because it requires them to do something.

Prophets see the vision which apostles are to build. I remember the Lord gave me a vision of a move of God. This was about a decade or more ago. I saw a vision of what could happen if we grabbed people together and went into certain towns with different gift mixes. I saw phase after phase of this movement growing and it was powerful! I tried to pioneer this thing, I bought a website, tried to get it going, but it never happened. Now it's a movement! I'm not a part of it but friends of mine run it. It looks almost exactly what was in my vision. At first, I felt like a real failure because I saw something and thought it was for me to build. In actuality, my job was to declare, "This is what God wants to do. He is shifting us from conference mentality to getting onto our horses again. He wants us going to a city and saying, 'we are not going to leave this city until God moves!'" The ark may have been for Moses to build, but this movement wasn't for me to build. It was for others.

Different Characteristics of Prophets

God is going to show you things and you may think you're supposed to build. Sometimes that may be the case. But remember, the prophet's anointing is on the words. As you speak the word of the Lord, there is an anointing for people to receive it and a grace is imparted to accomplish it.

Prophets are moved by inspiration. They live to see the Holy Spirit moving in power. The job of the prophet is to take the supernatural realm and make it a reality for everybody else. When you hear a prophet speak, it creates a hunger for the supernatural realm. Problems come when the church is fundamental, traditional, or for one reason or another has no grid for the supernatural. Prophets can't stick around stagnant pools.

Even spirit-filled churches can be exhausting for a prophet. As soon as they get to the service they're contending with whatever spirit is coming against the church that day. During worship, they may sense a door to breakthrough when others don't. A pastor or worship leader may skip right over it. It's worse when other leaders aren't prepared. Prophets are different from the other five-fold. They get revelation whether they're ready for it or not. Pastors and teachers have to prepare well beforehand in order to conduct the service. If they don't or if they try to wing it without the spirit moving on it, the prophet knows and has to contend all the harder.

I was speaking at a meeting in Canada and I had the worship team playing behind me while I ministered. I'm not that guy, but at one point I had to ask if they could do something different, change the key, play a different song. Something wasn't working. Finally, I approached the worship leader and asked if they could stop playing and just put on a worship CD. That could have been very offensive but after the service, he asked me, "How did you know?

"How did I know what?" He proceeded to tell me that just before they took the stage to play behind me, they had been in a full-on argument backstage. Instead of releasing praise and freedom, the worship team was releasing strife! That's why I couldn't minister while they played. Not because I just didn't like what they were doing, but because of the way prophets are wired: they're fueled by worship.

Worship is critical for every believer to get into the presence of the Lord. Everybody's called to do that. But because worship unlocks the supernatural realm, it's especially critical for the prophet. A lot of the prophets I know who are grumpy, their attitude is because they listen to way too much political news stations, to talk radio, or they're always listening to podcasts instead of pressing into worship. They still discern what's happening but they fuel it with negativity!

A favorite question of a prophet is, "Why are we doing this?" The church has a lot of great ideas, and some of them come from a sincere desire to see God move. It's not only prophets who want change. But the prophet doesn't care if it's a good idea, only if it's a God idea. "Did you ask God first?" They're all about change but that change has to come from God, not the wisdom of man.

Prophets absolutely hate religion. Religion is a form of godliness that denies the power. Worship might be happening, teaching might be happening, fellowship meals and church growth might all be happening, but the power of God is absent. The actions can all be the same but the heart is entirely different. That is why the prophet is constantly contending like Elisha did: "Where is the Lord God of Elijah? Where is the God of miracles?" The power of God uproots the religious spirit. As long as everything is safe and comfortable, some pastors are happy because they are building their church families. But prophets want to come and flip the thing upside-down! They want change at all times because they're always looking to what God wants to do next. Jesus told the multitudes that came to hear him, "Unless you eat the flesh of the Son of Man and drink His blood, you have no life in yourselves," John 6:53. That was Jesus operating as a prophet exposing the motives of people's hearts. He didn't care about numbers, he cared what was in their hearts. It's terrible having a friend who is a prophet if you don't want to change!

Prophets are Freedom Fighters

Religion creates conformity and prophets thrive in creativity. Conformity is like bricks: easy to build with but hard to make. It takes lots of pressure and control to get a brick. Once you've got bricks, it's easy to stack and build and swap out. But the bible doesn't call us bricks, it calls us "living stones" in 1 Peter 2:5. It's harder to build with a living stone. They're irregular in size and shape, and always changing! The important difference, though, is freedom. Freedom to be who they are in God. Prophets can't be bricks and they can't work with bricks.

You'll hear prophets say, "I hate the spirit of Jezebel," or "I hate the spirit of Absalom," because they hate control. A prophet will fight for you if you are willing to let go of whatever it is you have. They live to see God's justice on the earth. They see in black and white, no shades of gray. What's right is right, what's wrong is wrong. That's not to say this is how everyone should be. Remember, it's just how prophets are wired. Matthew 5:37 says, "But let your statement be, 'Yes, yes' or 'No, no'; anything beyond these is of evil." If someone tells me they'll do something, and they don't do it, my first thoughts are, "They're a liar! I can never trust them again!" I have to fight that part of my nature. When I respond like that, God comes to me and reminds me there is grace and forgiveness. Maybe they had the best of intentions and just got busy or forgot. Prophets have to be taught mercy, and that mercy and justice don't have to be in opposition.

It's because of this sense of justice that prophets often lead initiatives. Lou Engle is a prophet of God and his entire life has been gripped with the issue of abortion. God deposited an injustice in his heart that he will fight for the rest of his life. Prophets often latch onto one mission for their lives. You can discuss politics in front of a prophet and get no reaction. You can discuss culture and the prophet sits there quiet. But bring up the one topic the prophet has in her heart, and be prepared to see them go from meek and mild to roaring! You hit their justice chord.

If you tell a prophet you feel called to a certain cause but life's too busy, he'll likely smack you upside the head. They're wired to not let anything get in the way and they don't understand why others do. They don't fight for your freedom to be lazy, they fight for your freedom to pursue God with everything you are!

This intensity is the reason in Ephesians 4:11 it's apostles first, teachers last, and sandwiched in the middle are the prophets. Apostles and teachers deal in the objective word of God whereas the prophet deals in the subjective. He's guarded on both sides because of his intensity. Prophets live with very strong convictions and can easily offend and cause disruption without support. When you toss in the wounding of immature prophets, it gets more dangerous. Prophets must learn to grow and listen to others. Patience does not come easily to the prophet but it is a fruit of the Spirit and must be learned.

Prophets Call People Higher

There's the love of a pastor, which says God loves you just the way you are, which is true. Of course, the pastor wants you to live to your fullest but is at least pleased that you're showing up Sundays. The love of a prophet isn't content with that. He's concerned with justice, and justice is you living up to what God calls you to. A prophet sees your destiny and urges you toward it. Some people just like getting prophetic words. They attend a meeting, get another encouraging word, and add it to the other 57 they have sitting on a shelf they don't plan to do anything about. But if you walk alongside a prophet in relationship, you won't get off that easy. They love the people of God too much to let them stay where they are. "That's a great word! What's your action plan to make sure it comes to pass?" The Hebraic mentality is, "Esther, maybe you were raised for such a time as this but if you don't rise up, God will just raise somebody else in your stead." American Christianity doesn't think that way. Jesus said in Matthew 23:37-38 that Jerusalem had missed her time. We can miss our hour of visitation! God is faithful, though, and you can come back, turn your heart to Jesus and fulfill a little bit of what you were called to do, but ultimately it gets passed on to your children. Or like Acts 13:36 says, you can be like David and fulfill your purpose. It's hard to hear a scripture like that and not contend for people around you to accomplish everything God has for them.

Prophets want people to fulfill their destinies. People, however, don't want their comfort to be interrupted. A prophet can say to someone, "I love you. You know I love you, right? You're amazing. You good? Are we good? Okay. Because I've got some correction for you and I love you too much to let you go down this bad path you're on…" The receiver's heart should be to thank them and ask for guidance! Instead, prophets too often are blown off or pushed back. People don't want to be called out on their sin. Pride gets in the way. No one likes to be told what they're doing wrong, they don't like their secrets laid bare. And so, the prophet is rejected. Where God wants to bring change, freedom, and destiny, it all gets rejected.

"Well, if God told me himself, I'd receive the correction." He did tell you! He sent you one of his prophets! "If it's really that important, he'd tell me *directly*." Maybe he is and you aren't listening so he sent someone else to tell you. If you confess to honor the prophetic, make the choice to listen! But prophets, that's no excuse to forget humility yourself and exert control over others. Prophets hate being controlled but can fall into the same behavior in their efforts to raise people up. It's our job to *call* them up, not *haul* them up kicking and screaming. The prophet has to have the same heart that Daniel had when he ministered to Nebuchadnezzar who said, "Can you interpret the dream?"

"I wish this would happen to your enemies, great king. I wish this could happen to your enemies and not to you." He didn't say "I told you so!" The prophet has to understand that if you have not first interceded over an issue, then it probably isn't the time to say it.

You see the same with Nathaniel and David. My mistake in the past when I was growing in the gift was that if I saw it, I said it, whether or not I had relationship. That hurt people because they were like, "Why would God tell something so personal to someone not invested in my heart?" He was telling me so I could intercede! Not so that I could rebuke them and walk away.

If you have a reputation of giving harsh words, that's not the Lord: that's immaturity. You've been operating out of discerning of spirits and hurting people with whom you have no relationship. God gives you a word about someone so that you'll fall to your knees and cry out, "God, no!" on their behalf. "I pray for this person's brokenness, I pray for this person's understanding..." All of the sudden you're led to an encounter with the Father's love and you see the Father's heart for the person. Then, and only then, do you approach them with the word, if at all. Just calling out strangers does them no good.

People need to learn to receive the prophetic. On the flip side, prophets need maturity to walk out their gifting and calling so that people will receive.

Another reason prophets should be slow to release a word is that, in our desire to call people higher, we might release a word in the wrong season, or worse, the wrong word altogether. This is more of a problem for those with the gift of prophecy. There are those who come to meetings and *project* what they want to hear from a prophet. They shout out "Me, me, me!" when the minister takes the stage. Lo and behold, they get called on! In their mind they're screaming, "Give me a word about marriage!" The minister says, "I see marriage all over you." Yeah, because they were projecting and you picked it up in the prophetic realm. A prophet is going to see right through that. She'll stand back from the crowd and ask God, "Who do you want to speak to tonight?" I've been in meetings where prophets are asked to give words to everyone in attendance. "Everybody line up at the front and everyone gets a word from the Lord!" I used to do that but I was burning out. The Lord absolutely has a word for everyone and he'll get that word to them, one way or another. I'm more concerned with who specifically God wants me to talk to at a given time and place.

Personally, I'm slow to give a word because it comes with consequences. I'll be standing at the back of the sanctuary when I hear the Lord start speaking to me. I'll think, *Oh Lord, please speak to someone else. I love you, really, but please find someone else to talk to…* Then, of course, the senior pastor walks right up to me and asks, "Hey Ivan, are you getting anything?"

There's a real cost to giving a prophetic word. There's a lot at stake! When you realize people believe what you're saying and that they invest their hearts into the words—there's pressure! Friends call me and ask me to pray for them, to hear what the Lord is saying to them. I ask God and I hear him say something like, "Tell them to sell their business." *Augh! They're not going to like hearing that.* But they asked me. They invited me to speak into their life, and hopefully, they're mature enough to receive the word. I can't just deliver their mail and not have my heart invested. So I tell them.

"That's exactly what we've been feeling. Thanks!" *Phew! Praise God! That had me sweating.*

When I look at scripture, the kind of New Covenant prophet I most want to emulate is Barnabas. That wasn't even his real name. It was Joseph but they called him Barnabas which means "son of encouragement." Can you imagine bringing so much encouragement that people actually call you The Encourager? If you study the life of Barnabas, it is so amazing! After Saul's encounter and conversion, It was Barnabas who brought him before the other disciples to prove he'd really changed. Saul's life was in danger from all sides. I wonder what would have happened if Barnabas hadn't gone to get him?

Barnabas brought Paul out of relative obscurity. In the beginning of the journey it was Barnabas and Saul. Barnabas had to mentor Saul. Then you see and shift and suddenly it's Paul and Barnabas. Barnabas, a true prophet, knows when to step back because his function is to raise up other prophets. The immature prophet seeks the spotlight but the mature celebrate when it's another's turn to shine. Now Paul was an intense dude. When John Mark left them to return to Jerusalem, it upset Paul to the point that he didn't want together again for a time. Paul's not the kind of guy you would want as your pastor. But Barnabas saw destiny and value in John Mark and stayed with him.

Barnabas found people who were rejected; not the most prophetically attractive or the ones who wanted a word the most. He looked and said, "Who is the one God is working with right now?" Maybe they're in the back of the room and not trying to get the attention. They're the one who has gone through a season of intense brokenness which requires the prophet to come.

Look at Samuel and David. "Samuel is coming to your house! The most famous person in all of the land is coming over! Samuel the prophet, the judge of Israel!" Jesse lined up his seven sons and Samuel went down the line.

"Not you. Not you. Nope." That'd hurt our feelings, right? "Surely it is Abinadab. He's tall and handsome like Isaac. He's got the looks, the walk, and the talk. Surely this is the Lord's anointed!"

"That's not him, either," The Lord said. Samuel asked Jesse if he had any other sons. Why didn't Jesse invite David? There's lots of conjecture but whatever reason, he wasn't invited. Samuel called him out of that rejection. That's what a prophet does. The Lord spoke something to me when I was in my 20s. He said, "Ivan, I haven't called you 'David.'" *Ouch.* Everybody wants to be like David! He said, "I've called you to be like Samuel. Find David and anoint him king." My heart is to see the destiny in others and to fight for them harder than they fight for themselves. One time I was watching television and all of the sudden in the spirit I saw another screen appear in front of the television. A man was preaching and multitudes of people getting saved. The man then paused and said, "I just want to thank my spiritual father, Ivan Roman." The Lord said, "This will be your legacy." I don't care to be up front all of the time. I want to raise up people who will change the world. That's the heart of an equipper; that's the heart of a Barnabas.

Prophets desire to see everyone prophesying. "You don't feel like you have the gift of prophecy? Let me lay hands on you. Now prophesy to the person next to you. Yeah, just do it! It's easy! You don't see visions? Okay, BAM! Now see visions." This is partly because the prophet carries the impartation for it but it's also the heart of a prophet to see everyone seeing and hearing the voice of God.

Prophets Have The "Now" Word

Teachers and prophets can get really frustrated with one another because the prophet will announce, "This is the year of the harvest!" The teacher shakes his head because the bible says in John 4:35, "Do you not say, 'There are yet four months, and then comes the harvest'? Behold, I say to you, lift up your eyes and look on the fields, that they are white for harvest." The teacher is thinking to himself, *Jesus said that 2000 years ago, Mr. Prophet! Read your bible and you would know it's always harvest time!*

The the next year comes and the prophet announces, "This is the year of the open door! You are going to have opened doors over your life and you are going to be an open heaven! Year of the open heaven!" The teacher flips in his bible to Luke 3:21 and thinks, *when the heavens opened for Jesus he never shut them. We're always in an open heaven!*

They're both right. A Teacher has a theological understanding but the prophet declares what the Lord is focusing on in this season. Sometimes these prophetic words can evolve into theology. "Seek his face and not his hand" sounds super holy. But is it theologically accurate? Maybe some people, sometimes, need to seek his face above all else. But me? I want all of God! I want his face, his hands, everything!

Remember that the prophet has the now word. It's the right word for today might not be the right word to live by tomorrow. Stay close to God and stay close to the prophetic to keep moving with God. Scripture reminds us to ask, to seek, and to knock for a reason.

"Ask, and it will be given to you; seek, and you will find; knock, and it will be opened to you," Matthew 7:7.

"For everyone who asks receives, and he who seeks finds, and to him who knocks it will be opened," Matthew 7:8.

"So I say to you, ask, and it will be given to you; seek, and you will find; knock, and it will be opened to you," Luke 11:9.

"For everyone who asks, receives; and he who seeks, finds; and to him who knocks, it will be opened," Luke 11:10.

CHAPTER EIGHT

"Pitfalls of a Prophetic Person"

It's important to be aware of the pitfalls that prophetic people are at risk of falling into. The first to watch out for is the sin of pride.

Pride

It can be easy, when God tells you things before they happen, to have an attitude of, "I knew you were going to say that. I knew that was going to happen." No one likes a know-it-all. There's an early stage for the prophet when God speaks to you a lot. It's part of prophets training to prove God does actually speak and for you to learn to discern his voice. Some people take notes at church but I'd arrive with notes. I'd write down scriptures or topics God talked to me about in the morning then check my notes against what the preacher brought. Sure enough, they'd match. My wife and I would smile at each other, a little inside secret. But it can be easy to get a big head over this. Knowing things before others makes us feel important and can make us feel more important than them. It's a dangerous pitfall because, "Pride goes before destruction,m and a haughty spirit before stumbling," Proverbs 16:18.

Truth is, God doesn't tell us everything. I know an incredibly accurate prophet. This guy can give you a blueprint for your ministry for the next ten years and be spot-on. Who wouldn't want a word from a guy like that? Recently, I had the opportunity to give him a word. As I spoke, his hand went over his heart and he started to cry. "It feels so good to receive a word from the Lord," he said. He had words for everyone but still needed a prophet to speak into his own life.

We all are woven into the body of Christ, grafted onto the vine. We need each other. We need others to speak into us. 1 Corinthians 13:9 says, "For we know in part and we prophesy in part." No one has the whole picture. You may hear the voice of God but it is dangerous to take the stance of "God told me. I already know." There's a false mentality that says, "the Lord is my shepherd. I don't need anyone else speaking into my life." That's like holding your hands over your ears to further revelation. News flash: you're not the only one who hears from God.

Greed

The bible calls Balaam a prophet of God. The story goes that Balak, the king of Moab, asked Balaam to curse the Israelites. The guy was afraid of them because they'd conquered some of his neighbors and he thought he might be next. Balaam, for whatever reason, asked God what to do instead of immediately refusing the offer. God came to him and said, "Do not go with them; you shall not curse the people, for they are blessed," Numbers 22:12.

But then Balak offered him money. Balaam, who already had his answer from God, went back and asked again. "You sure I shouldn't curse your chosen people, Lord? This guy's offering me riches!" Numbers 22:20-21 says, "God came to Balaam at night and said to him, 'If the men have come to call you, rise up and go with them; but only the word which I speak to you shall you do.' So Balaam arose in the morning, and saddled his donkey and went with the leaders of Moab."

Let me tell you what I think was going on here. I feel like greed was already in the heart of Balaam. He had his answer from God but asked again. If God tells you what to do or, that is not the person you are supposed to marry or, don't move to that state or, whatever, and you keep asking over and over again, sometimes we hear the answer we want whether it's God's will or not. I call this prophesying through an idol in your heart.

"God, I want to get married! Is this person the one for me? She is, isn't she?"

The Lord says, "No! Cut it out!" Five minutes later, you're asking again. Eventually you ask so often it comes back to you as the answer! "God told me she's the one!" Maybe you even had a vision, but it could have been out of a soulish place within your own heart. Balaam heard, "Okay, you can go with them. But still don't do anything I wouldn't do." And Balaam, to his credit, prophesies blessing over the people, frustrating Balak. It seems Balaam did good. But skip to the end of the book and see what's written in Revelation 2:14. "But I have a few things against you, because you have there some who hold the teaching of Balaam, who kept teaching Balak to put a stumbling block before the sons of Israel, to eat things sacrificed to idols and to commit acts of immorality."

A missing piece to the story! Just reading Numbers doesn't reveal everything. It seems like the story ends with Balaam saying, "Though Balak were to give me his house full of silver and gold, I could not do anything contrary to the command of the Lord, either good or bad, of my own accord. What the Lord speaks, that I will speak?" And then in the book of Revelation you see the scripture and wonder what happened. It doesn't take much to assume that Balaam said, "Okay, I can't curse God's people. However, I can teach you the stumbling block that you can put before the people of God and then God will curse them." At the end of the day, the sin of greed motivated him to curse the people of God.

This kind of thing happens in the church today. Generosity is one thing. Sometimes I'll give a word and the person will be so moved they'll want to give to my ministry. That's great! There have been times when I have prophesied over families and they've come back later and said, "We want to sow into you – into your life and into your ministry." There's nothing wrong with that because it's generosity. But then there's manipulation. This happens quite a bit! When I travel, I'll occasionally get a message from someone, like a local businessman, asking for 30 or 40 minutes of my time. Wonderful. I'm happy to minister one-on-one, time permitting. I'll sit down with Mr. Business and he'll talk about the millions he's made and how much more he's about to make, and he's looking for a ministry to sow into. He just needs a little direction. If the word pans out... Who knows? You scratch my back, I'll scratch yours. It's terrible! I know places in other countries where they will bring prophets in front of very wealthy business people who pay top dollar for prophetic words. What happens is the prophet tries to conjure up a word that will get himself a bigger payday. Maybe it's totally false, maybe it's just putting a personal spin on a true word. Regardless, it's manipulation and it's prophesying from greed. Beware the sin of Balaam.

Rejection and Misunderstanding

We've covered prophets being rejected by people in previous chapters but it can go the other way, too. I've been at meetings and been a part of churches where prophets are stalked and hounded by people desperate for a word. I've been stopped in hallways by people asking for prayer. "Sure, I'll pray for you. What do you need prayer for?"

"Whatever the Lord says!" *Oh, you're asking for a prophetic word.* So I'd give them one. Then by the time I was done, a line had formed behind them! Not wanting to be rude, I'd pray for all of them. It was great, people were touched, but I was exhausted! And I felt more than a little used. This continued to happen. I've heard of prophets being followed into the bathroom or people somehow showing up at their hotel rooms asking for words. Eventually, the prophet is going to have enough of it. "Keep the people away from me!"

When I travel, I try to create a relational, naturally-supernatural culture everywhere I go. "You all hear the voice of God so I am going to minister only to a few people. If you still feel like you need a word, raise your hand and we are going to have some prophetic people pray for you. I am not the only one gifted." I ministered somewhere recently where I didn't really know anyone and couldn't operate like that, so it was just me, the prophet, functioning alone. Afterwards I got down from the stage and there was a line of people waiting for me. I thought they just wanted to chat! Nope, they were lined up waiting for a prophetic word each. I got back on stage, grabbed the mic, and said, "I hope you are not all here for a prophetic word! I thought you guys were just here to say hi to me and maybe pray for me or encourage me. Or maybe you need healing prayer. I'd be happy to pray with you for your healing. But if all you're asking for a word, that makes me feel so used!"

The room filled with the noise of disappointed sighs. I never did that when I was younger. I would minister to them while growing increasingly bitter. You see, prophets have to learn how to create boundaries. We don't need more bitter prophets! If you love yourself, you will have boundaries, even if saying "no" hurts someone's feelings. If I say no to one thing, I say yes to something else, and vice versa. If I say "yes" to praying for this line of people, I am possibly saying "no" to time with my wife and children. We are the only ones who can steward the life God has given us. Without those boundaries, prophets will isolate themselves from people, the very people they're supposed to serve. They don't want to interact because they feel used.

It was such a wreck at one point, I'd sit in my car outside the church and tremble in fear and anxiety. *I am going to go in there and 17 people are going to rush me and start asking me for ministry and I just can't take it.* It got so bad that I would hide in the bathroom during the service transitions when people might otherwise find me and pull on me for prayer. Prophets aren't magic 8-balls you can shake over and over for a word! We're people who need rest and ministered to ourselves.

Some people can't separate a prophet's function from relationship. If somebody who cares about you asks how you are, you might give them an honest response. "Not that good today, friend." But if a prophet asks, a lot of people get defensive. "Why? Why are you asking? What have you heard?" Their insecurities immediately come to the surface. This can also cause a prophet to feel rejected and therefore reject others.

There are prophetic types that look stranger than others. This strangeness can also lead to rejection. People don't like what they don't understand. Or they don't want to associate with the weird guy in the back of the room having an open-eye vision and speaking in tongues to himself. But think about this: the prophet operates out of revelation but most often delivers it through words. It's a vocal gift.

Many prophets receive love through the words of affirmation love language. They're constantly loving, blessing, and encouraging others, pouring themselves out. After a while, they're going to need to fill up again. Who will do that if everyone's rejected them or they've isolated themselves?

I've heard stories of high-level prophets who, after ministering to presidents and kings, would later ask friends who were with them, "Was that okay? Did I do okay?" You might say they needed a better revelation of their identity but I say maybe all they need are a few words of affirmation! We need to create a healthy culture around the five-fold ministry in which prophets have a safe place, where they won't feel like they have to isolate themselves.

Prophets and prophetic people often feel they don't fit in anywhere. They end up finding each other without solid teaching, without pastors, without apostolic vision. Then these fringe groups become so weird! They've all connected based on misunderstanding and rejection. Their gifts are still in operation but they've gravitated toward each other based on their hurts and continued to minister out of their wounding.

In 1 Kings 19:18, Elijah hid in his cave and said, "And I alone am left; and they seek my life, to take it away." He's isolated and depressed "I'm the only one who has this anointing! I'm the only one!" Then God said to that, "Yet I will leave 7,000 in Israel, all the knees that have not bowed to Baal and every mouth that has not kissed him." God basically said, "Get off of your high horse! I have 7,000 people just like you who have never bowed to the prophets of Baal. You are not the only one." Elijah had a victim mentality. "Nobody understands me. Nobody loves me. I'm all alone!" We see that a lot in the church!

Out insecurities can also cause misunderstandings. We all have insecurities, however there are individuals who are hypersensitive to what is going on in the spiritual realm. When they go into a room they are able to discern exactly what's going on. When I was young I went to my pastor and complained that I could tell people in the church were speaking against me. "Yeah, you're right," he said.

I said, "You pick it up too?"

"No. They came and told me." I demanded to know what we were going to do about it. "You're going to give them enough time to process in their own hearts before you confront them." All I wanted to do was confront them! However, it wasn't their fault I knew. Maybe given enough time they'd settle their grievance with me without me having to get involved!

If you're hypersensitive and somebody walks past, you might pick up that they're angry. Your insecurity, though, assumes they're angry at you. *Why are they angry at me? I didn't do anything to them! If they come and say something to me I am going to say something right back!* I used to have full-on arguments like this in my head. The Lord would come to me and say, "Would you stop it? You are hypersensitive because you are insecure. Your gift is really honed in. Sure, that person's angry, but probably not at you. Will you stop and pray for them?"

You might walk into a church and discern that there's a lot of anger or gossip going on. But your insecurity makes you think it's directed at you. This is why inner-healing is so important for prophetic people!

Ownership

Wounded prophets can be controlling. It's easy to give a prophetic word when you travel. You can show up somewhere, be bold, give all of these prophecies then leave. But when you are a prophet in your local church, a home group, or perhaps in your family, you have to face the people you give words to on a regular basis. That can get tricky! There's an inclination to think it's your job to make sure the word comes to pass so you can feel validated.

Instead of chasing people down later to find how the word is working out, what I like to do is dialogue with them in the moment. This isn't always possible with strangers and during meetings, but it's great with those you have relationship with. "Did that make sense to you? No really, honestly, don't just smile and nod. What did not make sense to you? Unpack this with me."

"Well, this and this and this made a lot of sense but this other thing didn't."

And so we talk about it! You may find yourself saying, "You know what? I think

I was wrong! I gave you a word and I really feel like I was wrong. Will you please forgive me? And will you please forgive any way that might have hindered your relationship with the Lord? I just wanted so much to see you step into this that I actually used my prophetic gift to manipulate you. And I am so sorry because that wasn't my heart." As we've seen, missing a word doesn't make you a false prophet. Prophets need to be open to correction, to admitting when they've missed it. When we have a high level of credibility in the prophetic, the prophetic wound in the church will heal.

Self Deprecation

I wrote earlier about a church that placed me in a position of eldership. They did that to replace someone else in the ministry, someone almost exactly like me. I heard stories about this guy. He was totally focused on truth and honesty. But, like me in my younger days, he didn't always do it with tact and sensitivity. He could be brutal! He was a prophet by calling but was mantled as a pastor, much like I am today. Some people in the church loved his pastoring style because he pastored as a father, prophetically seeing where they were veering off and steering them back. Others, though, hated his blunt nature. He'd call you out on your sin in front of other people! His heart was in the right place but his delivery lacked. He even prophesied the split of the ministry, the split that eventually led to my being there. It could have been avoided if the leadership listened to him.

I finally met him over breakfast. He saw me and said, "You're just like me!" We sat down and he asked, "Young man, do you find yourself apologizing all the time to God?"

"All the time!" He explained that as prophets, we live lifestyles of repentance. We are constantly repenting. He went on to say that, when pastors give poor advice, they aren't considered false pastors. But prophets are always in fear of being labeled false prophets. I've said it before: there's a lot of pressure giving a prophetic word. I mean, you're speaking *on behalf of God!* You take the stage to minister, all the while thinking, *I have to be perfect in my delivery; I have to be perfect in my message. Oh no! Did I do it right? Did I say the right things? Could I have said that nicer?* If you're not careful, you're constantly beating yourself up. This is why it's crucial for prophets to be in community, to be pastored!

Pastor-Prophet Relationship

Now, apostles and prophets get along for the most part. One has the blueprint, the other is a builder. It's a match made in heaven! But historically speaking, the pastor and the prophet have a little more tension in their relationship.

Why does the prophet need community? Because we are all members of a body. Prophets should belong to churches. The types of churches can vary wildly. There are mega churches down to house churches. Some house churches have 80 people, some have eight. The only thing that matters is why they gather. Some people get wounded at a big church and so swear them off. "I don't believe in big churches." Really? Solomon's Portico fit up to 700 people. It all depends on the mandate for that particular body. Called to build a mega church? Awesome! Called to hold church in a pub or bowling alley? Great! Just make sure it's God's idea, not man's. Prophets, though, can be critical of churches. "God's not moving there!" You sure about that? Maybe God has given a specific mandate to that particular senior leader to reach a different part of the community than you're called to. Prophets are seers, but their intensity can also give them tunnel vision. Find a church with a similar mandate to your own.

Your church should be like a family, a place that doesn't just use your gifting. They should care about you, not only what you can do for them. Bill Johnson uses an analogy of a bow and arrow. If you leave the string too long on the bow and never loosen it, it's ruined. You've got to have a place where you can relax and not always be *on* so you can avoid burnout. Relationship is critical. That said, a church that is all about family with no mission can be equally frustrating. The prophet is wired as a seer, to see what God is doing, help steer the people, and say, "The Lord is coming! Prepare ye the way of the Lord! This is what's happening!" If the whole purpose of the church is just to be a family, eventually the prophet is going to book it out of there. Family is necessary but it must have a mission! You want to know how church should look? Look at Jesus. He ate with his disciples but they also did things together. Not just bowling and board games; they turned the world upside down. Prophets need to be given vision. They need to be given assignments. They need to be moving constantly. The caution, though, is they can get so caught up in these things, they forget to do family, too.

Your church should also be a sort of hospital. A church should be a safe place for the wounded. It can't be all wounded, though. A healthy church is going to have its share of healthy people. Who else is going to take care of the wounded? If everyone's wounded, it's likely the leadership are wounded too, reproducing after their own kind. In a healthy community, everyone's at different stages. The church as a hospital is important so that the prophet who needs healing can receive that. But after they've healed up, they've got to be willing to stay and help others heal.

The prophet was never meant to live alone. 1 Samuel 19:20 says, "Then Saul sent messengers to take David, but when they saw the company of the prophets prophesying, with Samuel standing and presiding over them, the Spirit of God came upon the messengers of Saul; and they also prophesied." Samuel formed the School of the Prophets but we also see the School of the Prophets with Elijah and Elisha. We don't know exactly what the School of the Prophets was but the idea that prophets always dwelt alone is incorrect. Whether you're a prophet or not, God wants people together.

I remember one time I was working for a church where I was the only non-pastor. It was an all pastoral staff and it was always, "How is your heart? How are you doing? How is your family?"

Then I would say, "All of that is vitally important but when was the last time somebody got saved in this church? That's the reason why this church has been 50 to 70 members for 40 years! You have a really healthy little inner circle that no one else can come into. God wants to open to doors to the church! He wants to bring in people who are not saved! He wants to shift your leadership!" I got booted out. They wanted to protect their bubble. Later, though, God brought an apostolic leader in who shifted it from a small little church to 500 members! Eventually that guy moved on and the numbers sank back down. The old leaders didn't know how to build. Five-fold pastors need to partner with apostolic vision!

During that season I was dying spiritually because I couldn't share my journey with any of them. "I had a tremendous encounter last night!"

"That's great! Hey, are you up to date on your tithe?" They wanted to pastor me but didn't know how. There was no one I could take to! Then one day I got a phone call from a guy named Jeff Jansen. He said, "Hey! The Lord told me to call you! I heard about you."

"You heard about me?"

"Yep. What's the Lord been speaking to you?" God sent me someone who not only listened, but understood what I was going through! I told him I'd been having encounters under an apple tree in the spirit. Jeff said, "I've been living under that apple tree for two weeks!" *Wow.* "Do you know what it means?" He explained that God was inviting me to the secret place to hear him again, to hear fresh words from God. "Ivan, you're drying up. You're burning out. You are a prophet! What are you doing in that dry church? Come speak with me!" I ended up doing a bunch of conferences with Jeff. It was such a relief to minister with someone who knew what it was like to have crazy encounters!

The School of the Prophets, even if it's just prophets gathered together, is important so they can know they're not alone. "That's cool! Yeah, I saw that too! Whoa, I'm not crazy!" It can sound like I'm giving contradictory advice but both are true. Prophets need to be in churches but they also need the company of other prophets. They need the encouragement and companionship of similar giftings and the iron-sharpening-iron relationship with different giftings to create maturity.

The most common concerns for prophets or prophetic people about being pastored are:

1. Pastors don't understand me. They don't have the same experiences that I have. I can't go to my pastor and tell him that I am having angelic visitations or demonic visitations because they just won't get it.

That's not necessarily true! Even if they're not having the same experiences, they have stewardship from God, a grace from God for understanding, for love, for acceptance, and for nurturing. A pastor may not have the same experiences that you've had but a true father's heart is going to say, "That is so awesome!"

I have people in my life who I call after having crazy spiritual experiences. These are people I know and can trust to teach me. They process the encounter through the mind of a teacher and then we process it together. Other people I call just for encouragement or when I need someone to have my back. "That is so God! Ivan, I love it! Tell the world! And if they don't agree I will back you up!" Often these are older ministers, experienced men of God who've worn a path before me. They can tell me what the likely reaction to my revelation would be and offer advice. Both examples are pastoral relationships.

Another thing I hear everywhere I go is:

2. Pastors aren't spiritual.

Pastors usually focus on the heart and on the family; that's how they're wired. If God placed a pastor in oversight of a church then we have to believe he has given them the ability to lead the church! If you don't believe in the authority of that pastor then you shouldn't be there. If you can't submit yourself to the leadership of the church and you're going to constantly push against the goads, then you need to move on! The idea that pastors aren't spiritual because they don't have angelic visitations or visions—and I've been around five-fold pastors that do—is ridiculous. I remember one time I got prayer from a group of ministers. One guy prayed for me and it was like POW! I was knocked out by the power of God. Another one prayed and I got filled with the joy of the Lord! Then a man who identified himself as a five-fold pastor laid hands on me and I wept from the deepest place of my being. God ministered to my heart in a way that I didn't experience from any of the other five-fold ministries. I've been given prophetic words by pastors. Just because they're a pastor doesn't mean that they can't have a razor-sharp gift of prophecy. A pastor isn't going to operate like a prophet. "Hey you in the back, stand up! God has a word for you." Instead, the pastor prays silently, *Oh, that guy in the back. Father, touch them. I feel that pain. Lord, heal them.* They are interceding behind the scenes and getting a lot of the same revelation we do, they just don't have to do it up front. Their gift isn't as demonstrative as the prophet's.

Too often I've seen prophets, or any Christian really, bail when they clash with leadership. Listen, there are absolutely times when a leadership relationship is toxic and you need to get out of there. But a lot of the time, that tension is there to mature you. I grew up in New Jersey and for a lot of us, there's a sort of gang mentality of ride-or-die. "I'm a ride-or-die homie! I'm going to ride with you or I am going to die with you." The church is not like that! And yet we are supposed to be the ones to represent love! There are seasons in each of our lives where God will put us with leadership who will expose our hearts. If we don't allow this process, we go somewhere else and discover the same things happen there that happened at the first church. We never grow or mature!

3. The Pastor doesn't listen to my prophecies.

I hear this one a lot. Let me ask, are you trying to prophesy every single service? Are you emailing your pastor 37 pages, single-spaced, of every word you've ever been given? Are you trying to give a word seconds before the minister gets up to preach? Father, impart emotional intelligence to your people!

There's a process in church leadership. It's not just from God's mouth to the prophet's ear, to the pastor, and then done. If you give a word to the pastor for the church, don't expect him to nod, grab a mic and say, "I'd like to recognize prophet so-and-so who gave a word. We are doing it wrong. I just want to say thank you." No! What's going to happen is, if it's a genuine word from the Lord, it's going to bring conviction! Even if it's an encouragement. The pastor takes the word to the leadership, the core team, who discuss and pray over it. The one with the gift of the administration says, "We believe this is God but we don't have the finances. Let's contend for finances." Somebody else chimes in with, "I believe it's God, too, but there is timing." And the word gets processed and run through the proper channels. All the while the prophet is screaming, "Why isn't anything being done about the word?!" If you need accolades and pats on the back, that's your insecurities exposing themselves. As prophets, we don't shove words into the pastor's face and demand action. We submit them. That's part of the relationship.

4.   I'm not given a place to prophesy.

People have left my church, saying on their way out that they didn't feel they were able to prophesy. I mean, they were *able*, but they didn't feel like they were allowed. I'd respond with something like, "What? That's the opposite of my entire vision! Did you not understand the vision? The vision is a prophetic generation; a prophetic people! That's why we do classes and demonstrations!"

"Well, I mean, I wasn't given a place to prophesy at the front of the room. On stage."

"Oh. I see. God bless you on your search for a new church." They either didn't understand our core value that everyone can prophesy or they just wanted the spotlight.

If you feel you must be in the spotlight before you can prophesy, you don't belong in the spotlight. If you're in right relationship with your church and leadership, your gift will be honored. You won't need anyone's permission to prophesy! I was at Starbucks once with Tommy Green from the band Sleeping Giant. There was no line at the counter and the young woman was postured as if she really wanted to talk. I asked, "You like heavy metal music, don't you?"

"Yeah!"

"Hold on. This guy's famous." I called Tommy over and told him she liked his kind of music. I played her some on my phone then Tommy just started reading her mail. They spoke for a while then he sat down and wrote her a note from the Lord. I love that! He didn't have to say, "Pastor, can I have permission to prophesy?" That's not Kingdom!

5.   Pastors aren't sensitive to the spirit of the service.

I covered this already in the chapter on different characteristics of prophets. Because the prophet is spontaneous, it is the "now" word, what God is doing in the moment. There are times when we think, *Oh no! The pastor's missing it!* But are we sure of that? Sometimes we have to understand that the Lord may give the person in oversight some strategy, a plan that you don't know because you haven't been invited to that level of leadership. That's hard for prophetic people because they want to be in the know on everything! But maybe God gave special direction to the pastor and he's obeying God, only it looks to us like he's missing it. You may be picking things up in the spirit but it doesn't mean it is the mandate from the Lord for the church for that hour.

Let's turn it around for a moment. Here's a common complaint from pastors against prophets.

1. Prophets act like they're the only ones who hear from God.

It can be intimidating to be around someone who hears from God so clearly, so frequently. It can create a sense of insecurity where you stop believing you can hear from God. There is danger in comparing yourself to others. Pastors can absolutely hear God—they're one of the five-fold! Sometimes prophets can flaunt their revelation a little too much. Other times, it's the pastor's insecurity that makes him think that's what the prophet is doing.

2. Prophets are confrontational.

It's true, they can be. Immature prophets may feel that confrontation is a gift of the Holy Spirit. There's such a thing as healthy confrontation, a way to have brave communication. However, young, immature, or wounded prophets might feel like they have to come right out of the Old Testament, point their fingers and rebuke. That's not necessarily the best way to get your message across.

I've heard from a lot of pastors who've said something like, "Listen, we've got this guy. We believe he is a prophet and he's been accurate. But when I see him walk into the building I into another room because I just know he's going to come over to me and start giving me a word, tell me what I didn't do, speak about the church and all the demons there… It's overwhelming and I need a break!" That's a lack of emotional intelligence on the prophet's side. Just as important as receiving revelation is delivering it. Don't be a steamroller.

Some pastors struggle with using their experience or lack of experience as the plumb line. I remember a particular pastor said about prophets, "You know, I don't believe these people when they say that they see angels all of the time." This man was basing a belief on personal experience: because he didn't see angels all the time, neither could anyone else. Pastors, or anyone really, need to be careful not to compare how God speaks to them. Instead of being jealous or denying it happens, our hearts should rejoice that others experience it and our minds should want to investigate to learn more. Listen to the experience and try to understand even if you've never had an experience like it. If a prophetic person is in your church, and you believe in them and want to see them cultivated, shutting them down every time they say something you don't understand will quickly shut down the gift. That, or the prophet will move onto a ministry that values him.

If you're a prophet, not just someone with a prophetic gift but a real prophet, and the pastor doesn't make room for you, don't force it. The role needs to make a place for itself. It's not for us to force our way through doors we think should be open. Sometimes, though, we might see a closed door when in fact it is wide open. Some of the people I've struggled with the most have been pastors but only because of my own pride. I'd share with them revelations I'd received and they didn't seem to care! They weren't enamored with my gift! Only when I realized they cared more about my heart than my gift did I learn I could trust them with both.

The last thing I'll say to pastors about the prophet is this: create a safe environment for those with prophetic gifts. Don't allow the people in the congregation to pull on these people in an unhealthy. We've already discussed how this leads to rejection and isolation. It's partly the job of the prophet to establish boundaries but it's also the responsibility of the pastor to teach his church to respect the prophetic. The best way I know to do this is to create a culture where everyone prophesies. We all hear the voice of God. We don't need superstar prophets to hear what the Lord has to say. Need a word? Ask your neighbor. Ask the person sitting next to you in the pew.

I want to pray for the pastor-prophet relationship. They are both five-fold but rarely seem to work well together. That needs to change for the sake of the church.

Father, thank you for the five-fold ministers. Thank you especially right now for pastors and prophets. Lord, whatever rift exists between the two, heal it now. Heal the division. For the prophets, place someone in their lives who cares more about their heart than their gift. May they feel genuinely loved for who they are, not what they can provide. And for the pastors, Father, send them prophets with a full revelation of what it means to be a New Covenant prophet. Teach them to allow room for the prophetic so that your people won't perish for lack of vision. Lord, raise up healthy pastors and prophetic voices, and bring healing to your five-fold ministry. In Jesus' name, amen.

CHAPTER NINE

"The Prophet in Relationship with the Other Five-Fold"

Years ago, after I'd planted a church, a pastor who'd been in the ministry for 40 years sat down with me and the rest of the leadership. In the middle of the table, he placed this big, Coca-cola Christmas cookie jar. He then instructed us to write down what the jar looked like to us, stressing that we should only write exactly what we could see. When we finished, he asked me, "Okay, Ivan, what do you see?" I described the jar, telling him I could see Santa Claus, how he was dressed, and other details. The pastor said, "Wait a minute. What did you say you see? I don't see that! How do I know it's there?"

He explained, "The five-fold all see from a different perspective. It requires trust to not see what they see but to believe they see it. It takes all five-fold to see the whole picture."

This exercise had a huge impact on me. God has given each of these other ministries a part of his heart to see the church. There is no division within the five-fold ministry by design but instead unity and harmony when all the pieces work together.

If you're reading this, you likely have a basic understanding by now of who the five-fold are and how they act and operate. Put the five of them in a church staff meeting and it will go something like this:

The apostle says, "How do we impact the city? I love our local church be we need to think bigger. We need to think city-wide transformation. How can our church be a training and equipping center to raise up an army to send to the outermost parts of the earth?"

The prophet says, "All I really care about is what God is saying. What's on God heart for our church in this season? Give me three or four days to get alone with God and I'll come back with a vision for our church."

The evangelist says, "Why are we still here? We're in a building with air conditioning and comfy chairs and the lost are out there dying! They are going to hell in a handbasket while we're in here in a staff meeting eating cookies! Come on people!"

The pastor says, "What about the people? How will the decisions we make today impact the people in our care?"

The teacher says, "What about the word? Are our people grounded enough in the Bible to carry out this vision? What are the scriptural precedents?"

These ministers are wired a particular way for a particular reason. They were made to work together but it doesn't happen automatically. That's also by design. These five need to be in right relationship with each other to function at their peak. There needs to be trust and that doesn't happen overnight. When there's no relationship, I've seen them jostle for position and fight to have their own way. That rarely ends well.

Characteristics of Healthy Five-Fold Ministry

A healthy, mature apostle functions as the church visionary. They pioneer movements. They are also able to gather people around a cause because they have a father's or mother's heart. They want to raise up matures sons and daughter with global vision.

There are two different models. First, there's the Jerusalem Council model in which everyone *gathered* to Jerusalem. It's a gathering place where you come together to be restored and to get the word of the Lord. Then, there's the Antioch model or the Acts 13 model. This is the *sending out* model. "While they were ministering to the Lord and fasting, the Holy Spirit said, 'Set apart for Me Barnabas and Saul for the work to which I have called them.' Then, when they had fasted and prayed and laid their hands on them, they sent them away," Acts 13:2-3.

The Antioch model identifies giftings in the body, identifies where they will be of the most benefit, and sends them, even though it could be a loss to the local body. There is sacrifice but there is also joy in people fulfilling their destiny.

My wife Erica and I met with a church planter once. At the time, his ministry had planted about 500. At the time of this writing, it's over 1100 churches. Their model is to grow through home groups. Someone in the church would start a home group and once it got to a certain size, a new leader would be chosen and the group would split in two. Once an original home group had spawned a certain number of others, leadership would approach and say, "You've successfully grown this many home groups. It's obvious to us that you have a five-fold calling on your life. If you are willing, we as a movement will support you. You can stand up in our church," which is massive, by the way, "announce that you are going to plant a new church, and that anybody who likes can go with you. Not our staff or team, but anyone else can go with you. Not only that but we'll give you the financial support to make it happen."

We were told that a lot of people follow. Sometimes a few hundred will choose to go and help plant a church. That's a serious void left behind! But you know what happens? It always gets filled back up because the church sends out its best. They know how to minister and grow. The apostle at the helm of this ministry understands that he's not there to build his own kingdom but God's kingdom.

My personal experience of being around apostolic leaders is that they make you feel like a giant. There's something they carry, confidence and humility, that rubs off on you and you think, *I can take over the world!*

Healthy prophets carry a zeal for God! There's a desire in all of the five-fold, but specifically among prophets, to be on the cutting edge as a reformer or change agent. That's because it's in them to be exactly that. If prophets played baseball, they'd play shortstop. "I've got to be where the action is!" At their best, they're also encouragers, seeing the best in people.

Healthy evangelists love the broken. They also tend to be fun. They've got to be charismatic in order to attract the lost to them! You catch more flies with honey than vinegar, as the saying goes.

Evangelists, when all healed-up, impart faith. Complain around an evangelist about how you've been struggling financially and they're likely to say, "Let me pray for you! Let me impart my faith because I believe that God can do big things! We serve a *big* God!" Bob Jones used to preach on the five-fold using the hand. The thumb is the apostle because it touches all the others. The evangelist, though, is the middle finger because it has the longest reach. They have the most faith! It's because of the nature of evangelism; they have for multitudes to come to the Lord.

The pastor has a genuine love for the church. Healthy pastors have a love that extends in all situations. Babies are still adorable even when they mess in their diapers. Similarly, pastors see all people as lovable, despite their mess. It's their fatherly or motherly nature.

A healthy five-fold teacher is a lot of fun to talk to because of the information they offer. You can ask any question you like about the bible and if they don't already have an answer, they'll be excited to search one out for you. Teachers, in my experience, are motivated by freedom because if you know the truth, "the truth will set you free," That's their desire for the whole world, to shine the light of truth for everyone.

Characteristics of Unhealthy Five-Fold Ministry

Unhealthy, immature apostles who turn away from the Lord have the ability to start cults. They still have the gift and calling that are without repentance. They still have the ability to gather people together under a vision. The challenge with an unhealthy or immature apostolic leader is that they will build on vision alone without relationship. Their goal becomes simply to be bigger, to be more. They lack a father's heart which makes them very controlling. There tend to be a lot of empty promises. Then, without relationship, anybody associated will eventually feel used just for their gifting and part ways with the apostle.

Some apostles are just so weary of prophetic words that haven't come to pass that they refuse to hear another one. "I've had word after word that revival is coming to my region and it hasn't. These weren't small-time prophets, either. I'm just over the whole thing." Scripture has a warning for this. 1 Thessalonians 5:19-20 says, "Do not quench the Spirit; do not despise prophetic utterances." It's my conviction that if we want the fire of the Holy Spirit moving in our lives then we need to embrace the prophetic. But a wounded apostle may shut out the prophetic because he blames it for his hurt.

If you've read the whole book up to this point, it's probably easy for you to imagine what an unhealthy or immature prophet is like. One time, I'm not naming names, I was in a meeting listening to a prophet minister. This guy was at least twice my age and the Lord gave me a word for him. I hesitated because I didn't want him to think I was giving him a word just to get close to him and talk with "the man of God." I snuck over and said, "Excuse me, sir, I don't mean to distract you but sitting over there I felt like the Lord gave me an impression."

He just looked and said, "What is it, young man?" I proceeded to tell him what I heard the Lord say. His countenance changed and he looked at me like the proudest papa ever. He then spoke prophetically into my life and it was with such love! However, a woman came up behind us and stood there, hovering. Soon the man looked at her and said, "Yes? Can we help you?"

She said, "I want you to do for me what you're doing for him!"

"Excuse me?!" He said. Gone was that sweet spirit of love he'd spoken to me in.

She pressed on. "Well, I want a word!"

He said, "I've got a word for you! How about process? Here's another word. Patience! You obviously lack that!" He called her out and he wasn't gentle about it. It was hilarious but terrible! The poor woman began to whimper. He looked at me and said, "Young man, never let anyone take advantage of your gift like that!" There were probably better ways to handle that situation. But that's how a wounded prophet can act. Their gift is still in operation but they can use the sharpness of it like a knife.

Speaking from personal experience, when I'm not feeling well, or when I'm stressed or something is going on in my heart, I can become extremely critical. I need to be extra careful to stay in worship and not to make any major decisions.

A critical spirit is not the same as discerning of spirits! A discerning of spirits gift can see the negative but it is an invitation to hear God for what He is saying. With a critical spirit, everywhere you go and everything you see is negative. It creates isolation or rifts in relationships. If there's no redemption to what you are seeing, then it is not the testimony of Jesus Christ! Jesus is all about forgiveness! Even Jezebel was given time to repent. Sometimes prophets get so cranky, after a while they can get like, "God is done with this city! I'm shaking the dust from my boots!" Well, that prophet is done but God's not done!

Unhealthy, immature, wounded, and otherwise broken evangelists hate the church. They don't want to have any part in it. They see the church as a bunch of lazy people to criticize. Any form of organized church is garbage! Their hearts are still for the broken and disenfranchised but it's hard to help them when you're one of them! You can't bring peace to a people when you have the same struggles they do. So they stand on the sidelines, criticizing everything about the church instead of being part of the answer.

Wounded and unhealthy pastors, like apostles, can be very controlling. Or they fall to the other side of the spectrum and become very non-confrontational. Confrontation, done well, is an important part of the journey. Iron sharpens iron! If you fear confrontation, either get healing or get out of ministry! You're in big trouble if you can't have healthy confrontation. You need to be able to look someone in the eye and say, "No." Especially as a spiritual father or mother. A wounded pastor lets his children walk all over him.

Pastors can receive wounds easily because they love so deeply. They have a deep desire to gather people together but aren't always great at releasing them. When a family leaves the church, regardless of the circumstances, it can seem like rejection and all sorts of thoughts run through their minds. "Hey, friend! I love you! Haven't seen you in a while. What've you been up to? Oh. God called you away. You're at the church up the road? Oh. Well, that's great! God bless!" *We had coffee and meals together. I so wanted to get to know you better. I wanted our children to grow up together. I did your grandfather's funeral! I officiated your son's wedding! That meant something to me. That time you were at my home and we wept together. I thought it was more than just ministry. I thought we were becoming family...* Some people review churches like restaurants. "The service was meh. I'd give it a two out of ten." The pastor feels that! They invest their hearts into people only to be rejected by so many. Understand that pastors are wired to feel things very deeply. They need to guard their hearts but the church needs to be careful to take good care of their pastors. If their hearts become too hardened, they become controlling. And in a hardened, closed-off heart, it's difficult for the Holy Spirit to move.

Teachers who are unhealthy or immature are the know-it-alls of the body of Christ. They tend to be wise in their own opinions and they have an opinion on everything! Like the evangelist, they become hyper critical. They point out others' flaws and inject their own views as gospel, not merely a difference of opinion. They feel the need to correct everything and everyone.

These teachers are argumentative instead of receptive. A good teacher should be like the Bereans, who "received the word with great eagerness, examining the Scriptures daily to see whether these things were so," Acts 17:11. They heard Paul's message and, instead of arguing with him, did their research to see if he was right. They had teachable spirits! A teacher should always maintain a teachable spirit.

Healthy Relationships Between the Prophet and the Other Five-Fold

As a prophet, something in me can sense when I'm around a genuine apostle or apostolic ministry. I have this mental picture of a prophet and an apostle with huge smiles high-fiving each other. It's that kind of relationship and energy. It's very easy to submit to and it happens without me even realizing.

The Prophet in Relationship with the Other Five-Fold

The apostle as the spirit of wisdom and the prophet has the spirit of revelation. Without revelation, there's nothing to be wise about and without wisdom, you don't know what to do with the revelation! The prophet sees, but the apostolic has the ability to lay the foundation. In 1 Corinthians 3:10, Paul called himself an *architekton*, or "master builder."

Lou Engle prophesied The Call for years. What you may or may not know is it was made possible in part by Ché Ahn, an apostle who came alongside Lou to make The Call happen. He helped pull together the vision and the laborers to bring the prophetic word into reality. A ministry run just by a prophet will have a lot of zeal and passion, and of course revelation, but not a lot of commitment. The prophet is always on to the next initiative. "What's God saying *right now?*" The apostle grounds the prophet and keeps everyone productive.

When attached to a healthy apostle, the prophet feels like she's at Disneyland! There's so much freedom to be who she is and to operate how she was designed because the vision is so big. A prophet will be willing to lay down their life for an apostle who honors and allows room for their gifts.

Prophets and Teachers are both focused on the Word; one on the *rhema*, the spoken word of God, and the other on the *logos* or the written word. In a healthy relationship, the prophet will release a word of God and the teacher will share scripture to confirm it. They're not pitted against each other. In fact, prophetic words should always be backed-up by the written word! Teachers are necessary to keep the people in line, or rather *aligned* with the true gospel message. If the prophet starts to go a little sideways in their subjective handling of the word, the teacher can pull him back. Likewise, the prophet can remind the teacher that God's word is alive and that he still speaks fresh revelation to his people.

Teachers can also expound on what prophets bring. A prophet may bring a word, a few sentences or a few paragraphs, then the teacher can latch hold and bring further clarification. They can develop whole series of teachings off of what the prophet brings!

Prophets and Evangelists come together over the harvest. Prophets release

God's heart for times and regions. This often concerns the lost which is where the evangelist steps in. The evangelist hears the word of the Lord and steps in behind with faith to bring in the harvest. It's sort of like throwing darts at a world map. God aims the dart, the prophet throws it, and the evangelist puts boots to ground wherever it lands.

It can work the other way round, too. I've been called by evangelist friends who've been in meetings and who've said, "These meetings feel different. They're unique. Will you ask the Lord what he's saying and doing here?" They're eager for an opportunity to save the lost. They're just as spiritually sensitive as the other-five fold and need the prophetic gift for direction. One time, after being asked this question, I prayed and the Lord spoke to me about fire and glory. I saw fire and oil being poured out in Fort McMurray, Alberta, Canada. I told my friend what I saw and the word was released. A day later, oil fires spread through that city. Now, I don't believe the actual fire and destruction was God's doing. It was the enemy's counterfeit. God was releasing spiritual fire and oil in the region. The believers in the area could be comforted by the fact that, although the enemy had brought destruction, God was bringing his own fire and oil and it was a confirmation to their hearts they were supposed to stay.

We've already spent a lot of time on the relationship between prophets and pastors but I will say one more thing. Sometimes, God will use a prophet to protect a pastor's heart. This happens to me occasionally that I'll get excited when new people come to the church. What pastor doesn't love visitors? I'll shake their hands, maybe they tell me how much they liked the service and I'll begin making plans with them right away. Later, the prophet will pull me aside and say, "They won't be here long." Or, "The Lord says their foundation isn't strong enough, so don't build on them." It's not that the prophet, or God for that matter, want the pastor to ignore those people, they just don't want the pastor's heart wounded when they inevitably leave.

What about a prophet's relationship with other prophets? That's just as important as the ones previously mentioned. I discussed in a previous chapter the school of the prophets and the benefit of being around similar gifting. In a healthy community, there shouldn't be just one prophet but a prophetic roundtable. If you've never been a part of this kind of thing, it is so incredible! The encouragement that comes from learning others are hearing the same things you do has immense value. One prophet shyly says what he saw and another chimes in that she saw the same thing. Then a third confirms and says, "Don't you know, in the Hebrew, this is the year of the…" And suddenly it's like popcorn, words and confirmations popping off around the room. It feels so validating!

There are those who want nothing to do with the five-fold because they've only experienced it when it wasn't functioning like it's supposed to. An easy example is the Shepherding Movement of the 1970s and 80s. Leadership thought the church was full of sheep that needed constant control. You want to get married? Talk to the pastor. You want to buy a car? Talk to the pastor. You want to make any decision at all? Talk to the pastor. It wasn't all bad but the temptation was there for ministers to go on power trips, and a lot of them did. If you grew up in that, you might not like the idea of an organized church leadership. Or worse, you might be afraid of it.

Others simply struggle with unbelief. "You think apostles and prophets are still around today? I don't buy that." Maybe they grew up in a church that taught cessationism, the theology that tongues, miracles, and prophecy ended when the original apostles died. And some people just don't believe in the five-fold ministry as a concept. Still others have seen it forced where it didn't belong, like square pegs in round holes. Bobby Conner once said to me, "We're reading the sonogram, trying to determine the baby's gender weeks before it's even possible." What he meant was, people are trying to identify the five-fold where it's too early to tell, or where it doesn't belong. Some churches, in their zeal to adopt it, make it up as they go. "Five-fold ministry is coming! But who is it? I'm the pastor, that one's easy. Uh, you! You hear God. You're the prophet. And you have vision so you're the apostle. You, the greeter. You're kinda good at talking with people so you must be the evangelist!" That's not how the five-fold ministry works!

Five-fold ministry is birthed by God. In this new Apostolic Reformation, we must learn to identify the giftings in one another. We need to embrace healing and work towards wholeness. We should communicate, have open and honest conversations, and establish relationships built on trust and mutual respect. We must be able to say, "I trust you to see what I don't see."

It's coming. The five-fold is re-emerging and I am so excited to see it happen. The church needs to be careful during this transition to make sure it isn't just about the gifts but relationships. This same invitation has been extended to previous generations and I don't want to miss it again. When we understand that our identities are in Christ, as sons and daughters who are loved by Abba Father, and not in our abilities or callings, we'll be able to accept and hold onto the invitation. There'll be no more jostling for position but instead, we'll be propping each other up to reach higher heights. We'll begin to recognize the different anointings that lie on the people around us and we'll go to them for what they've got. Not to use them but to find wholeness with them. The body of Christ can and will operate as one!

That's community. That's what I'm longing for! And I hope you long for it, too.

My admonition to prophets is this: start off with a solid foundation and never forget your identity. I have found in my 17 years of ministry that the enemy would love to challenge my identity all of the time! Your identity is found in Luke 3:21-22. "Now when all the people were baptized, Jesus was also baptized, and while He was praying, heaven was opened, and the Holy Spirit descended upon Him in bodily form like a dove, and a voice came out of heaven, "You are My beloved Son, in You I am well-pleased." Then, in Luke 4:1-4 we read, "Jesus, full of the Holy Spirit, returned from the Jordan and was led around by the Spirit in the wilderness for forty days, being tempted by the devil. And He ate nothing during those days, and when they had ended, He became hungry. And the devil said to Him, "If You are the Son of God, tell this stone to become bread." And Jesus answered him, "It is written, 'Man shall not live on bread alone.'"

If Satan attacked Jesus' identity then how much more will he attack ours? It's vital that our identities are continually founded in sonship, in the word of God, and in relationship with God. As prophets, I highly recommend that you become inner-healing junkies! You should absolutely love and embrace inner-healing so that your hearts become so tender to the touch of the Holy Spirit.

Father, I thank you for what you are doing with this fresh awakening and how you are breathing on the prophetic ministry. And God, I thank you for these prophets you are raising up. Establish for each of them a solid foundation of identity and sonship. May they never grow beyond the revelation of Abba's love! There is no greater revelation than "the Father loves me!" Whether operating as a prophet or as a janitor, the revelation that God loves us is all that matters. In Jesus' name, Amen.

INTERVIEW ONE

"Erica & Ivan Roman: Married to a Prophet"

Please introduce yourselves.

Erica: Hi! My name is Erica Roman and I've been married to Ivan for 12 years. We have three boys, ages 11, 9, and 7 and we live in Medford, Oregon.

Ivan: My name is Ivan Roman and we're going to answer some questions about being a prophetic couple and being married to a prophet.

How did the two of you meet?

Ivan: Well, I moved to a small town in Oregon and was attending this church where there was this really attractive girl. A prophet called me and he said, "Ivan, where do you live?"

"Grant's Pass."

He said, "That's right. The Lord says you're just passing through."

I knew I wasn't going to be there very long so I didn't want to get involved in any serious relationship because I didn't want to hurt anyone when I left. Then, when I saw Erica, I felt something on the inside and I asked the youth pastor, "Do you know that girl?"

"Oh yeah, Erica! She helps with the kids."

I said, "Keep me away from her!"

"Why?"

"I'm attracted to her and I know that I'm not going to be here very long."

Erica volunteered with the youth, the church would bring me in to speak, and then I started hanging out with the youth pastors which gave us mutual friends. It was basically love at first sight! Is that about right?

Erica: Yeah, your side of it, sure!

What's the real story here, Erica?

Erica: No, I mean that's true, just his side. I didn't know he liked me. He didn't give it away at all! He was just this really nice guy, and handsome, and we hung out with the same group of people. I would never have known.

Ivan: I've got to share this. There was a little bit of a reputation because I had traveled with Todd Bentley and he had been a part of this church and he was very well known. Then I was a student at Bethel and so I had kind of this ministry reputation. When I moved to this small church, people treated me very differently. I didn't like it. When I started hanging out with Erica, she'd pick on me! She was hilarious and she just didn't care about where I'd traveled or who I had traveled with. We were able to build a real friendship. Because of the way people were treating me, I wanted to be around somebody real. It was really attractive to me that she didn't care about the Christian superstardom nonsense. She cared about integrity and all that good stuff.

What's it like being the wife of a prophet and itinerant minister?

Erica: I think for any wife you care how people treat your husband. You want people to treat them with respect and you want them to feel valued. I think sometimes, the people on the road, they use him for his giftings without thinking of it like that. They're just thinking about themselves more, what they'll get out of his being there. I think they should go to the Lord for themselves and ask those questions instead of overstepping bounds with a prophet. They need to wait on the Lord. And sometimes that waiting is the hardest part because you want God

152

to tell you what to do right now. So when you learn that someone is hearing from the Lord, and you hear these really accurate words they're giving people, you think, "Oh! I have to get my word from him and then everything is going to be great!" I've seen people, one after another, take Ivan's time where they really should be hearing for themselves.

Ivan: That's a great response! I think initially when God opens doors for ministry, regardless of what your five-fold ministry gift is, your heart is to serve people. You genuinely love people and you want to pour into them, and there is this kind of naive expectation that people are just going to treat you with respect and honor and take care of you. Early on in the itinerant ministry world where the gift of prophecy began to operate through me, people would line up to receive a prophetic word and it was honoring because they wanted to hear from the Lord. And so I would pray for people—but it was never enough! And then it was more people, and more people, and more people. The side that people don't see is what happens when the minister comes home exhausted, wiped out, and doesn't have anything left to give to his spouse. There's a facet of ministry few people talk about that the Apostle Paul calls the "work of ministry." It is work. It is a job. I have a job to come and release a message, to release what the Lord has for you, to minister to people. But there is a certain place where you're tired, you're exhausted, you're fatigued. You're human! Even Jesus often withdrew to be by himself to pray. And so I think that boundaries are important.

But even then, in ministry, you'll always feel pulled on. There will always be someone who pushes through the crowd when you're exhausted and announced ministry is done for the night who will say, "Will you pray for me? I have cancer!" Well, how can you not stop and pray for that person? It's not an issue of not having compassion; it's an issue of being a human being who ultimately can't fix everyone's problems. When your reputation grows as someone who is credible and so on and so forth, then people come to you not just for a word of encouragement but for some very specific things: "Should I leave my husband?" or "Should I move and go to Africa?" or "Where is my lost child?" Things that are like, "Whoa!" That is not the kind of pressure you put on any person! Ultimately, if the Holy Spirit has a word about that he will bring it. But I think people really do have to get back to what Erica was saying and have a genuine, authentic relationship with Jesus, hear his voice, and learn patience and waiting on Him just like everybody else does.

Erica: That's why I think Ivan's heart and message are so important, that we can all hear his voice. And God wants to speak to us! That was such a revelation to me. It's not just about being saved and being a good person who follows the rules, but now you're telling me that not only do I pray to him, which is talking to God, but now he can actually speak back to me? It changed my life! Just know that you can have a relationship with God changes everything! One of my favorite things is for people to hear the Lord's voice for the first time and know that he loves them.

There are people who've walked their whole life knowing the Lord and loving Jesus but they've never heard his voice. They didn't know that the Holy Spirit could be so close to them. If I didn't have him leading and guiding me, if I wasn't able to speak with him and commune with him, I don't know what I'd do. I don't know how people do it in their marriage without that! Early on in our marriage, I remember praying, "Lord, what do I do?" I had never met anyone like Ivan before. Our personalities are so opposite. There was a lot of adjustment! So it was just so great to know that I had the Holy Spirit with me.

You have opposite personalities but you're also both prophetic. How does that work in your marriage?

Ivan: The Lord will speak to me, whether it is through his voice or an encounter or a dream, and I get the feeling it's going to happen immediately. I'll tell Erica, "God spoke to me and said that we're supposed to move!" Or, "The Lord spoke to me and said the ministry is going to be like this..." I started to think I was missing it because it would take two to three years before anything would even happen. I was missing the timing. Since we married, Erica has always been the timing piece. Now when I hear the voice of God and share it with Erica, there are moments when she'll say, "That's the Lord! We need to do that! That's now!" Other times, because she has a really strong gift of wisdom, she'll say, "You know what, honey? I think you're right. I think this is the Lord, but I feel like it is two to three years from now." She's really been like the rudder to the ship or the anchor to my prophetic gift.

Erica: We can all hear God. The whole body of Christ is called to be prophetic. But Ivan walks in the office of a prophet. I don't want to generalize for everyone but a lot of prophetic people seem to be extremely passionate about the words they get. And like Ivan, they think the words are for right now and there's no room for error. They're seriously intense and they don't understand why everyone else isn't just as intense and aren't just as excited as they are. I think that's why God brings them helpmates, to say, "It's okay! Let's pray about timing. Let's pray about this."

I didn't grow up with in the prophetic culture so this was all new to me. I didn't know where to learn about it other than to pray. "Okay, God. What do I do with this?" The thing I probably prayed for most was wisdom. I can't imagine the pressure on Ivan, getting words whether it's for people or regions, and know when to release those words. Early on, he would just tell people whatever it was he saw and let them deal with it. But now he doesn't do that. If he's going to give somebody a word, he's going to be invested in them. And so as a wife, I'm invested in him, helping him. Prophets are hard on themselves. Maybe it comes from rejection or people not receiving the words like you thought, or not seeing things happen when you think they should. They can feel misunderstood. For my part, I'm there to say, "It's okay. I understand." Other people don't. They don't know what is going on or what he's feeling.

Ivan: Concerning the timing piece, what I would share with young married couples is the—and I've apologized to Erica profusely for this! There were times I said, "God told me we are doing this, so we are doing it!" Not like I was abusive or anything but it was very much this urgency that "We need to obey God!" I didn't even bother asking her what she thought. Now, Erica loves Jesus just as much or more than I do! She hears his voice. Early on in our marriage this counselor sat with me and said, "Ivan, the Lord is going to use your wife to speak to you."

I remember saying, "Meh. I'm the one who hears the voice of God!"

I'm just being honest! I look back and if I had just waited for the Lord to speak to her, the timing would have been way better. Or we would have been more *together.* Sometimes, that urgency you feel as a prophet where "it has to be done now," needs to be tempered. It needs to be tempered with someone like my wife's personality—she's steady like a rock! I tend to ride the rollercoaster and she is just steady all of the time. That's my advice to other prophetic couples. "It's okay! You're not going to miss it! Chill out a little bit, you know?"

Erica: Prophets can also be hard on the church. I've seen where they categorize themselves as prophets first, church second. Like they have this idea they are the special ones, the anointed ones who hear from God so they can exclude themselves from the church. I'd just like to remind them that, they are the church! You have to love what Jesus loves as much as he does. You can't beat up what Jesus loves. That's one area I've seen Ivan really grown in. He has the ability to really love people and to make them feel loved and valued and listened to. It's easy to give someone a word and then walk away. It's hard to walk alongside them to see the word come to pass.

Ivan: Isn't she a phenomenal communicator? It's because she's a teacher. It's true that I travel and I have a prophetic ministry but when we come home we don't disengage. I don't shut off the prophetic just because that's my job. It's a lifestyle. It's not just ministry. That's the thing I want people to hear. It's not just the prophetic for a ministry. This is our way of life.

Erica and I put a lot of stock into our prophetic dreams and what we're hearing from the Lord. And because Erica is so careful when she has a direction, whether it be for our ministry, our lives, or the church, I trust her 100%. I don't question it. A lot of the time when people in the church come to me and say, "That was a great decision for the church," I just say, "That was Erica's revelation!"

Erica: It is our lifestyle, and we do take the prophetic seriously, but prophetic people should take time to have fun and to have hobbies. Otherwise, you get a little stressed out I think, and that was one of the major things for us. There has to be some kind of other outlet. That doesn't mean you put Jesus in the closet. I can see Ivan's wheels turning and I'm like, "Okay honey, you need to go have some fun!" I'm always encouraging him to hang out with his friends. That's just as important

156

as spending time with God, reading your bible, preparing messages, whatever. It's important to do life. Each one of us is unique and special and God put gifts and creativity into each of us. He likes to have fun with us! I don't think people realize how much that he just likes to have fun. Setting time aside for that is as important as setting time aside to pray.

That was missing from our marriage for a while. Ivan would go from one meeting to the next meeting to the next and it was just too much. Too much of the same thing.

Ivan: Prophets tend to be futuristic and you're always thinking about the destination. "What am I going to become? What's my calling? What's the will of God for my life?" Hobbies can seem like a waste of time in that mindset. But then you start having kids and you realize that the love language of a child is fun and play, and kids learn through play. God really used my kids to chill me out a little bit. I think it is important for all of us to recognize that when you study the will of God in scripture, it is not so much about what you do as it is about who you become. The Bible says that the will of God for you is your sanctification. 1 Thessalonians 5:16, "Rejoice always!" This is the will of God for you. Too often, we're so busy looking ahead for the will of God that we miss the moments we're in right now. Life is about the moments.

Jesus is my destination! Right now it is all about my time spent with Erica and the kids. I think for prophetic people there needs to be an understanding that the future is in God's hands. I really had to work hard at learning to be present.

I was just thinking of something funny with the boys. One time my son got in the car, I think it was Aaron, and he was really quiet and wouldn't tell me what was wrong with him. So I said, "If you don't tell me, I'm going to ask the Lord!"

He said, "Yeah right, Daddy."

So I touched my son and said, "Something happened at school. A kid picked on you."

He told his brothers, "Don't let him touch you anymore! Don't let Dad touch you! He reads your mind!"

Interview with Erica & Ivan Roman: Married to a Prophet

Erica: That was a funny joke for a while.

Ivan: It was a funny joke for a while. I remember one time, this is because Erica was just talking about hobbies, but once I had a vision of Jesus and I doing Jiu Jitsu and he was wrestling with me. I didn't want to wrestle back because he was Jesus! I was having a hard time wrestling with God but the whole time he was playing with me. Just playing! He spoke to me, like, "I want to do Jiu Jitsu with you!" I was feeling guilty about leaving Erica and the kids to do something I loved but that didn't involve them. I love Jiu Jitsu but I felt guilty about making time for it. I was thinking about it one day when I told my son, Isaiah, "I had a vision that Jesus and I were doing Jiu Jitsu."

He said, "That's awesome Dad!" I thought, *Please don't tell anyone that your Daddy just said that!* That has to sound weird! Then I go into churches and I have an open vision and I see what God is doing and I think, *What are our kids going to be like having us as parents?* What a different way to raise your family! What a different way to live!

How do you raise your children in the prophetic?

Ivan: Let me start and then I will hand it over. When Erica was pregnant, I remember the Lord would speak to her about each kid and she would write it in a notebook. We had an agreement that if it girl, she could name the child, and if it was a boy, I could choose the name.

Erica: Because I was so sure that we were having a girl, I thought, "Sure! You can name all the boys. No problem!" I lost that bet!

Ivan: My father had a dream and in the dream, he saw a boy with curly hair. He said he looked just like me and that his name was "Isaías" which is Spanish for Isaiah. I thought that was interesting but I really didn't think too much about it. One night I was washing dishes and all of the sudden I heard it! "Isaiah!" And so I said, "Erica! I think I just heard the name for our boy! It's Isaiah!" She got up and ran to the room and pulled out the notebook. Inside, she'd written "Isaiah" and she had scriptural references. What I so appreciate and value about Erica and her prophetic gifting is that she really has led our family, our children, by the voice of God. She saw things ten years ago, their interests and what their personalities were going to be like, that have come to fruition. She saw things about musical interests and now our boys are doing guitar lessons. She's done a great job.

Erica: Thanks! I wish kids came with an instruction manual. Even when you hear the voice of God he doesn't necessarily give you details on everything. But it's kind of cool, I mean, who better could you ask than your Father in Heaven? "Okay God, I don't really know what to do with this child that you've given me. What should I do about this situation?" That's one of my favorite things that I love about Ivan. Sometimes I'm like, "Okay Ivan, I've been with the kids all day. I don't know what's going on with this one. He's having a meltdown. Could you just pray and ask the Lord?" And even though he's been gone all day, he'll pray and then know what's wrong and how to take care of it. That's an amazing parental hack! Just pray and God gives us the answer.

What I love about children is that it is so easy for them to hear the voice of God because they don't know any different. If you tell them to pray, ask the Lord a question and that he can answer you, they believe it! And they really do hear an answer or see a picture in their minds. I wish I had that when I was little. They don't know how amazing it is they haven't had to grow up without that. It's so fun! We've had the kids on trips and they just see what their Daddy does. They see what Mommy does, that we pray for people. And they love praying for people. Two of our sons love to pray for healing. It's like their favorite thing. One always asks Ivan if anybody got healed at his meetings. Our oldest son, he loves praying for people's hearts. He is such a sweet, compassionate boy that way. They all are, but when he prays it's amazing what God shows him. And he has just such the confidence! He's definitely Ivan's son.

We'll be at the table together and Ivan will say, "I had a dream" or "I had this vision." Our oldest, Isaiah, you would think he was not even paying attention, like he's looking at his plate or playing his video game, but he'll say, "Oh Dad I know what that is!" In an instant, he'll know the interpretation of the dream or vision. And it's perfect! Before I can even process what Ivan said, Isaiah already has the interpretation! It's so encouraging as a parent to see your kids moving in that direction and loving the Lord and knowing his voice. It's just so natural for them!

Ivan: I don't think it's just because Erica and I are prophetic. We've really leaned on the Holy Spirit for our family. Both of us. We've prayed for our kids because we had to! You would never guess what our middle son used to be like. He used to be shy because he has an older brother with this big personality and a younger brother who, as the baby, gets all sorts of attention. His personality sort of faded into the background. So the Lord put it in our hearts to have more one-on-one time with him. We do special days with just him and I. Dad time! We've been doing that for years. Now he talks almost more than his siblings.

Erica: It is so interesting how he went from this shy person, and then one prayer gets answered and he calls himself "awesome" and is super-confident in himself. I just love that about him! I'm like, "Look at this kid! That is all you, God!"

Ivan: Proverbs 22:6 says, "Train up a child in the way he should go, even when he is old he will not depart from it." Not the way that you want them to go. I mean, we want them to go in righteousness but in the context of that verse, it's calling, what God has put in their hearts. So Erica and I talk a lot about who our kids are becoming and what we can recognize in them.

My older boy is really prophetic and probably will end up doing what I do. I've seen him read people's mail. He's had encounters where he has seen Jesus. He's seen angels. I mean he's hungry for that whole realm.

What's some other advice you'd give to prophetic couples that you wish you'd had going into your marriage?

Ivan: I remember early on in our marriage Erica had a prophetic gifting but I was already traveling and doing ministry before I met her. When we were newly married she would get super-accurate stuff but then I would operate in the Naba flow. For her one minute of revelation, I'd have six. She really struggled with that for a season. But over the years what we've discovered is she brings the missing revelation I don't have. When we pray together for people, I might be seeing destiny, future, calling, etc. Then Erica will see the simplest thing but they'll lose it and start weeping because she spoke directly to their hearts, to their very beings.

So, I would encourage prophets to not view your spouses as not as spiritual as you. And for the spouses of prophets, don't compare your gifting. It's a slippery slope. You've been paired for a reason, to compliment each other. Erica has ministered to me more than any other minister! And I think to the spouses, understanding that you do not have to be as gifted. What people in ministry are looking for people around whom they can let their hair down. They also need to be kept grounded. I'll return from a ministry trip where I was a celebrity for the weekend and now Erica is telling me to take out the trash. That's good for us! And encouraging your spouse brings such tremendous breakthrough! For me, Erica is "home." It doesn't matter where we live. She creates an atmosphere that I love coming back to. It's where I can be goofy, I don't have to perform, and we have fun as a family. I see too much competition in marriages. It needs to be a safe place, where husband and wife and genuine each other.

Erica: We're in it together!

Ivan: Right!

Erica: No take-backs.

Ivan: No take-backs. Erica's father, when he was walking her up the aisle at our wedding, he looked at me and said, "No take-backs!" That's our philosophy.

In conclusion, prophetic people; make the voice of God more than a ministry. It's more than a platform to build your ministry. Lean on God's presence to strengthen yourself, your marriage, and to help raise your children. Sometimes the Lord will tell me that I need to check the oil in my wife's oil. He doesn't just want to talk to you about the big things, about city-wide revival. The little things matter just as much. It comes down to sonship. One of the main things I've learned is to carry the presence of God and the voice of God in every facet of life. Don't leave it behind after the meetings are over.

Let's pray. Father, thank you for the married couples reading. And for those who desire a spouse, I would encourage you that instead of asking for a spouse, ask the Lord to make you the right person for that spouse. We just pray right now in Jesus' name that marriages would be healed and restored. Lord, Erica and I pray an impartation of what you've placed on our lives, even our journey of growing and learning to walk together. How can two walk together unless they agree? I pray that even as Erica and I have learned how to walk together in life and in ministry, that you would impart that to those reading. Father, I pray that eyes would be opened to see and ears open to hear and that you would just release fresh revelation in every aspect of our lives. We ask this in Jesus' name. Amen.

Erica: Amen!

INTERVIEW TWO

"Patricia King"

When did you know you were called to the office of a prophet?

I got a prophetic word in August of 1978 from a credible prophet about a prophetic calling; a very clear prophetic word that God was calling me as a prophet. When that word came I believed it was true but I didn't know when it was going to manifest. I believed it because of the credibility of the prophet but also because I could feel the anointing on the word. I never activated it. Of course, I was active in the prophetic but I never identified myself as a prophet except in agreement with that word. It was years later in 1997 or 98, I was in the Netherlands speaking at a conference and the spirit of the Lord used me. I could feel the authority and I could feel the Lord speaking in the meeting. There were over 2000 people there and you could hear over the loudspeaker the sound of a man's voice agreeing with me. But the men in the sound booth couldn't figure out where the voice was coming from. After that session, I definitely knew the Lord had used me. I definitely knew that it was something from outside of myself and it was something that I had never felt before.

The leader of that meeting approached me and said, "I would like you to travel with us. We are going to be traveling all over Europe over the next year and I would like you to join the tour with me and I would like you to bring a prophetic word for each city." He had identified the prophetic authority I had ministered in during that meeting.

I said, "This is a first for me. I have never operated in that level of authority before and I don't want to disappoint you if I come."

He said, "No, I really feel that you are to come." Then I felt the Lord say yes, and my husband released me to go, so away I went. But on that tour, I couldn't get any words, I couldn't get any sense, I felt like I was just flopping city by city by city. I could tell that the man who had invited me was disappointed. We ended up and a church where the pastor had been the interpreter for me in that big meeting in which I had prophesied.

I went into his office and I said, "I just feel like such and failure. Now I have about to go and prophesy to your church and I just don't even know if I should be ministering."

He got a prophetic word from the Lord and said, "10 years ago, you received a prophetic word about your prophets calling." I shared with him the word I'd received in 1978. He said, "Why aren't you operating in it? The reason why the authority isn't released is because you haven't taken ownership of the call. I am not going to let you leave my office until you say, 'I am a prophet.'"

I told him I couldn't do that. He asked me why. I said, "Because I feel like it would be presumptuous. I am waiting for the Lord to reveal the timing on that and the grooming for that."

He said, "He has already declared it over you, you just haven't been released into it because you haven't taken ownership. So I want you to say, 'I am a prophet.'" But I just couldn't do it. We sat there for over an hour and he wouldn't let me leave. He refused to even start the meeting until I said it. He said, "I feel really strong in the Lord on this." So, I finally spit it out. It was one of the hardest things I have ever done. But after I had released it and said that I was a prophet, something shifted. I could feel it. For the rest of that tour, I was able to receive words. They didn't carry the weight that they had in that initial meeting but I knew something had shifted. This internal confidence was established in me, knowing that I was the eyes and ears of the body of Christ. I realized he wanted to deposit things from heaven into the earth; threads of revelation of who he is, almost like the sons of Issachar who discerned the time and place and knew what Israel should do. And he wanted me to introduce those things. Things like prophetic evangelism, and his glory and the supernatural.

I started getting visitations from the Lord, downloading insights and revelations concerning what he wanted to impart to his church at that given time. As he gave them to me, I would just say, "Yes." Then I would declare those words through teachings and prophecies. I would put them up on the Elijahlist. We would develop teachings and curriculum and videos. We did everything that we could to get that word out. Then we began to build small apostolic models for the prophetic word as well. We built models for prophetic evangelism and for the glory in a context that church communities could see and understand what they looked like. And of course, we used media to fuel that message.

I don't get a lot of prophetic words like maybe other prophets get. I get mainly words about what God is wanting to deposit. Right now I am getting a word regarding women and I have been carrying this word for a few years now. Usually, the words I carry have the duration of 7-10 years because it takes time for them to saturate the body of Christ. During that time, many people will begin to write and prophecy about the same thing. God has his prophets build and declare and reveal until it is established. The mandate of the prophetic word for women has been a few years now. I am prophesying women into their place, into their calling, but also because God's spirit is specifically pouring out on women in order to bring the men into their place that he established in Genesis 1:28 where it says, "He blessed men (men and women) to be fruitful multiply and fill the earth and have dominion." He shared with me that we are not going to see the fullness of that kingdom authority without men and women being in that place because it's on both male and female. The two of them have to come together. Because of that word I've been carrying, I have built a women-in-ministry network for people to nurture women into their place to stand in the fulfillment of that word. If you look around, you'll see women's networks emerging and different messages being spoken about the spirit of God being poured out on women. Even in the world, women are fighting for equal wages and equal treatment. In the sports world, too. That is the type of prophetic ministry that I mainly walk in. It says in Amos 3:7, "Surely the Lord God does nothing unless He reveals His secret counsel to His servants the prophets."

When you received the word from the prophet in 1978, do you believe that, if you had made the declaration "I am a prophet" and come into agreement with the word at that time, the mantle would have come on you then?

That's a hard question to answer. I feel that when a prophetic word is given it's not a guarantee. It is an invitation and potential. Within that is the journey. For example, there was Joseph who dreamed a prophetic dream that his family was going to bow down to him. Joseph definitely took ownership of what the dream was speaking but it wasn't the right timing for it to be revealed.

That is a big question in my heart. What that the prophet said to my heart that day was, I received a prophetic words so many years before, why hadn't I acted on it? It wasn't activated because I hadn't taken ownership of it. But I want to be clear: that's not necessarily the same for everyone. Sometimes there is a timing and a maturity where God will reveal something to you and then he puts it before you like he did with Joseph. Joseph had to grow into that word. There was also positioning for that word to come to pass. He had to be positioned by the Lord and it was in the Lord's timing to be fulfilled. The way it happened for me isn't the same way it will happen for others.

When you receive a word, first of all, there's agreement. You have to come into agreement with that prophetic word. You also need to check that it bears witness with your spirit and then agree with it. That is what puts that word into motion.

Second is Prayer. You have to be like Elijah who placed his face between his knees. We have to pray through the word. Or like Anna the Prophetess who knew the messiah was going to be made manifest in Israel. She prayed into that for 60 years, from the time she understood the prophetic word until she saw the fulfillment with her own eyes. A lot of times there is a journey to fulfillment.

And third is, Fulfilling the Conditions. For example, on the particular day when that prophet said to me, "until you take ownership of that word, until you say 'I am a prophet,' then this word will not be activated in your life." I had to obey the word of the Lord at that time. Then when I finally did obey, things started to open up.

Can you talk about the mantle you walk in? Maybe give some examples of the hats you've worn in your journey. What seasons has God brought you through since receiving the word in 1978?

In the makings of a minister of the gospel, the first thing you have to understand is that you are a son or a daughter. A child of God. Therefore the first mantle you have, when walking deeper with God, is to walk as a child.

The second thing you have to understand is you are a servant. But you cannot be a servant until you know that you are a son or daughter. Otherwise, you will be serving out of the wrong mindset. The reason I can serve well for my father is that I know that I am a daughter first. I am not a slave, I am a daughter. A lot of the roles that I walked in a maturing process until this day are those as a servant out of knowing that I am a daughter. I have served other people's ministries, in administration, in the ministry of helps, in evangelism; everything that I have put my hand to, I feel like I have done as a servant to the Lord as a daughter.

One of my largest foundational areas of service as a new believer, even after I received that word in 1978, was that of an intercessor. Be faithful in prayer behind the scenes where no one else is looking. Be a worshiper when no one else is looking. Serve other people's ministries when no one else is looking. Not for the purpose of getting promoted. I don't think that Joseph ever served as he did with the intention of promotion or gain. I think he did his best unto the Lord in the station that he was in. If he was in prison or if he was in Potiphar's house, he was faithful to the calling of the Lord on his life at that moment. There are lots of things every individual is called to do along the way and no task is too small. I've taught Sunday school. I've cared for children at risk. I've worked in the medical field and cared for the sick. I think all of that contributes toward the sensitivity of hearing the Lord's voice. All of them build, not only character and faithfulness but experience. Every realm we work in becomes useful to us as we grow. The more we grow, the more our capacity to understand the ways of God grows.

I was a cook for a season in Belize in Central America. My husband, my children and I were joined by an evangelism team there. We thought we were there for one reason but, when we got there, we discovered they had other plans for us. I was assigned to be the head of the kitchen. There was no running water, no electricity. We didn't even have a budget for food. We had to believe God to provide food to cook. It was a real big learning curve, and it was really something where we had to check our attitude before God and before man. When I look back now, it was like a leadership training school, learning how to lead by serving how to believe God for everything that we needed.

How does God normally speak to you? How do you hear his voice?

I think everyone has a way that the Lord speaks to them more, but I think other ways can always be developed by reason of practice. For me, I sense things more than any other way. I will sense in my spirit a green light to move forward on something or I will sense in my spirit the Lord's purpose. But also I get a lot of impressions when I am in prayer or when I'm seeking the Lord's voice or a word in particular. I will get lots of pictures and symbols and things that I need to seek the Lord further on. I do hear the still small voice very often. It is one of the most common ways that the Lord speaks to me We should all learn to identify that voice. It's like, I have been married to my husband for over 45 years and if he comes through the garage door I know it's him and not anyone else. Other people have access to our garage and our home but I always know when it's him. I know the way he opens the door, the way he walks, the way he breathes. If he were to stand behind me and breath I would know that it's him. The reason why is that we have lived together that long. When you do life together with God you get to know his voice and his whisper. Even though I've had open visions, I've had dreams and trances, I've heard his audible voice, all of that, for the most part, I hear him in the faint impressions, senses, and thoughts.

What word of wisdom would you give to people who have the calling of God on their lives, to mentor them along their journey in the prophetic?

I always want them to know what a privilege it is to serve the Lord; to be one he has chosen to deliver his word. It's not to be taken lightly. Something that has concerned me over the years is when I see people using the favor that comes with the calling (because your gifting will open doors and make room for you) and when the favor increases, they forget that it is the Lord that calls you by name. And the prophet, one of the five-fold ministries which were designed to equip the body of Christ, must always remember that the body belongs to the Lord. That body is not to serve you; you are to serve her. If you are called as a servant of the Lord you are to lay down your life just as Jesus laid down his. He is God and he became a man to serve us, and even though he was God he didn't consider equality with God a thing to be considered. He emptied himself and became a bond servant. The one thing I want anyone I mentor to know is that the people you are serving are not for you. You are for them. To extract your well being, your self-esteem, and finances from them is wrong. I've seen it too often amongst ministers; reaching into people's pockets to line their own. Do you understand who you are serving? You are serving God primarily but he sent you to serve his people. Not to rape his people. Rape is when you take advantage of someone with things that belong to them. They don't belong to you. The bride does not belong to us; the bride belongs to God. If people who are walking in their calling would humble themselves before God just like Jesus did and become bondservants, they'd realize that you don't touch the bride of the Lord for yourself because she doesn't belong to you. It's a very high and holy calling.

INTERVIEW THREE

"Shawn Bolz"

When did you feel called to be a Prophet?

I had a hope when growing up that I would be in the ministry but I wanted to do some other stuff too. I didn't know I was a prophet until the day I was ordained as one so I didn't take the title seriously. I was building prophetic communities where I was, helping people connect with the gift of prophecy in the body of Christ and around the world. But I don't know that I even believed in the five fold ministry at the time.

I began to grow in my understanding of being called a prophet. I realized that everyone could have a prophetic gifting but then there are people who help inspire that call. There are some that get assignments from God that deal with the government of agencies, the government of churches, the foundation of businesses and entertainment industries. God consistently gives these assignments to those who have a prophetic gifting or calling of a prophet and I realized probably 15 years in that, "Oh my gosh, I'm fulfilling the role of a prophet."

I was part of a prophetic community but to me, it didn't feel very biblically real. I don't know if I hadn't quite caught up to the theology or I was a little bit of skeptic. Even though I loved everybody in that community, it just felt strange to me. I grew up as an air force kid and I called all the generals by their first names because my dad was a colonel. Protocol was something that I always kind of rebelled against.

Now that I understand the call of a prophet in a biblical sense, I understand how it begins to build a framework. You don't have to be bound to protocol but it helps to bring definition. It helps to partner and participate differently.

What can you share about your prophetic journey?

I had parents who believed in hearing from God and it was just a part of our normal family life. If you lost your keys, you'd ask God where they were. Even during our schooling, we would ask God what sort of electives we should take, what kinds of lessons we should take, and what would develop us as human beings. We asked him what was in his heart for us. How do we partner with God and include him in our lives and everything? When I was in junior high and high school, we were in a little bit of a revival and a lot of the salvations I saw when evangelizing were because I prophesied over them. I'd say one statement that I heard from God and they would open up their whole heart. I didn't even know at the time that I was prophesying. I wouldn't say, "This is a prophecy." I would just say "God is showing me..." or "I feel like this...", or "I am having a spiritual feeling..." All the sudden, things happened.

When I was 19, I went to Los Angeles to pursue musical theater. As it ended up, God called me to a ministry in Kansas City, which was one of the places where the prophetic was really known at the time. But at that time it had died down. They'd actually let go of all the prophets on staff. It was becoming more of a mainline vineyard church. When I got there, it was actually kind of boring. I was thinking "What!? I gave up musical theater for this?" I wanted to go after something real. I'd read stories about all the people that had been there prophesying and said to myself, "OK, let's recreate some of those stories. Not the prophetic identities but the prophetic culture where we all can prophesy." I ended up being ordained a prophet there and stayed a part of that prophetic movement for 12 years. I also worked with a ministry called Rock the Nations which came out of Lou Engle's the Call. There were some other ministries that I was involved in where I held a prophetic role but I was focused on what it would look like to transform culture. Seven mountaintop mandate kind of stuff. Transformational theology. That was my passion, to see society transformed, but I was being used in the prophetic to bring in that transformation. Out of that, God began to build this prophetic identity in me so I could understand how to hear his voice and be in alignment in order to bring transformation.

Now, I understand how to operate under that authority so I ended up aligning myself with Bill Johnson and Chris Vallotton at Bethel Church in Redding, California. These are such amazing men and are great examples of how to bring transformation into an area. They've helped me to fine-tune some things that I wouldn't have focused on for myself but I knew I was being obedient to God.

How does God speak to you? How do you normally hear his voice?

I feel because I was raised in the church, in the charismatic culture, that I share a lot of headspace with God. I read in 1 Corinthians 2 where is says, "The Spirit searches all things, even the depths of God." He also searches the deepest parts of man, and those things tied together gives us the mind of Christ. The usual way I receive revelation is through impressions and downloaded thoughts where I share his thoughts. Originally I thought I wasn't speaking prophetically but I learned how to discern and understand that's not me, that's God bringing impressions or thoughts to me. So I think with him and get his heart for things. You'd pay a lot of money to know the thoughts of a billionaire, of a president, of the most successful people ever in ministry. And here we have the thoughts of God!

I've had visions. I've had encounters and some wonderful prophetic experiences. Those were not things that I could have ever made happen or made up. As far as sharing and having faith in God, it's usually very organic how I receive revelation. When I'm reading the bible, the scriptures get highlighted and I become aware of God in my thoughts. It's in that mediation between God and me, in the presence of the Holy Spirit, that I'm reminded our spirits are connected.

Can you share stories about how you've prophetically ministered to people outside the church?

172

One of my favorite stories that I don't really talk about that much is was when I was in an Asian nation. While there I made a kind of judgmental statement about one of the major corporations in that country. A worldwide and well-known corporation. It was something like, "They hardly ever give anything to the poor. How long can God bless a company that is taking such a high percentage of the economy of the world without giving back?" It was so weird because I was just making a statement, a kind of a political statement, without realizing that I was actually prophesying. The daughter of the CO was there at the meeting. She came up to me afterward and invited me to dinner with her and her husband. My translator encouraged me to go, saying they were really neat people. I ended up going with them down into a sort of panic room through underneath their house. In the room, there was a couple sitting at a table across from us. I was then told they were Buddhist. The woman who invited me played the recording of what I said about the company. They looked like they had been crying and said that everything I had said was true. They asked "Is God going to judge us. Is He going to take our company from us because we have been so greedy? We haven't helped the world. We haven't helped in education or children at risk. All the things that you said. Are we coming under the judgment of God? Does God hate us?" I remember thinking, "Dear Jesus, how did I get myself into this situation?" I that moment I felt like the Lord showed me, "Here's why I created them and this is what I want to do in and through them." He showed me where they'd gotten off track, then he showed me their true north and how to bring them back into alignment. The entire time they were recognizing what the Lord was saying to them as true and they repented. They said they didn't want to be that way anymore. It was almost like I had become a spiritual life coach to them. That year, after our encounter, they gave 10% of the corporation's income to education and children at risk. The next year they gave 12%. Then their corporation got into one of the two biggest markets in the world for their type of work. God reminded them that he gave them what they had and that they needed to come into alignment or he'd give it to someone else. They needed to hear that but I would have never said it on my own. It was almost like God tricked me into saying it because I thought I was just expressing an opinion. God designed it to go into the hearts of these people in this major corporation who were like kings in their industry.

Here's another story. I was on a plane and the woman sitting next to me was devastated because she was going through a crisis in her life. She asked me, "What do you do for a living? I'm going to a funeral and it will help me take my mind off things." I began to tell her that I was a Christian minister. She said, "Oh, I don't believe in God. Tell me about everything that you do." I shared with her about who God is, even in the context of her life. I told her what God could do for her. All the while there were prophetic undertones to everything I was saying to her. Then she began to prophesy to me. She didn't understand what she was doing but she told me, "You should be on TV," and other things that were in alignment with my calling. I said to her, "Do you know what you're doing? You're prophesying. Come on, prophesy!" She didn't even believe in God and ended up prophesying the heart of God. She opened up and began to share what was going on in her life and her call to Hollywood. Through this experience, she was able to come into an understanding of what her life was about. She never really had that Father's voice to help her along in her journey. There was no understanding how to embrace the things she was called to. She was at war with her calling to Hollywood and her identity because she was always in her dad's shadow and it was like the prophetic nurtured and mentored her to understand her identity.

What would you say to an emerging prophetic voice? If you were mentoring someone in the prophetic, what would tell them?

Fall in love with the people that you are going to be ministering to. Don't let it be about you; let it always be about them. Don't get self-absorbed. Don't get self-interested. Do care about the person you're prophesying to. Whether they're homeless or a king, if you love them, there's faith to prophesy. Fall in love them; even before you get to them. Pray that if God will give you an audience with his people that you treat them like the family. Treat them how you would want someone else to treat your closest family member. You want to be that person who nurtures them. The Holy Spirit is a counselor and a friend. He's a confidant. You want to be that when you minister to people. Help them feel like they are home with you. For me, the biggest mistake prophetic people can make is when they get so ministry focused that they forget the actual people that they are ministering to. God wants to entrust prophets to say things to his people that only a friend of God can say. Love is the primary goal.